Betty Crocker's
BEST
Bread Machine
Cookbook

The goodness of homemade bread the easy way.

Macmillan • USA

MACMILLAN GENERAL EDUCATION USA
A Pearson Education Macmillan Company
1633 Broadway
New York, NY 10019-6785

Macmillan Publishing books may be purchased for business or sales promotional use. For information please write:
Special Markets Department, Macmillan Publishing USA, 1633 Broadway, New York, NY 10019.

Library of Congress Cataloging-in-Publication Data

Crocker, Betty.
    [Best Bread Machine Cookbook]
    Betty Crocker's Best Bread Machine Cookbook.
        p.   cm.
    Includes index.
    ISBN 0-02-863023-8 (alk. paper)
    1. Bread.   2. Automatic bread machines.   I. Title: Best bread
machine cookbook.
    TX769.C735 1999
    641.8'15—dc21   99-12272
                                                                 CIP

GENERAL MILLS, INC.
Betty Crocker Kitchens
Manager, Publishing: Lois L. Tlusty
Editor: Lois L. Tlusty
Recipe Development: Karen Blanchard, Maria Ingall, Phyllis Kral
Food Styling: Betty Crocker Kitchens: Food Stylists
Nutritionist: Nancy Holmes, R.D.
Photography: General Mill's Photographic Services

Cover and Book Design: Michele Laseau

For consistent baking results, the Betty Crocker Kitchens recommend Gold Medal Flour.

Manufactured in the United States of America
10 9 8 7 6 5 4 3 2
First Edition

Cover Photos: Oatmeal Sunflower Bread, page 82; Fiery Four-Pepper Bread, page 32

Dear Bread Lovers,

Enjoy the old-fashioned aroma and goodness of home-baked bread made the fun and easy new-fashioned way—using an electric bread machine! It is the easiest, most convenient and modern way to make bread today. Whether you let the bread machine do all the work or you add the final touches by shaping and baking the dough in the oven, there is no better way of sharing love than with freshly baked bread.

We tested hundreds and hundreds of loaves of bread, rolls and coffee cakes in our kitchens. Whether you're an experienced baker or just getting into baking bread, we hope by sharing our testing results with you that your bread baking experience will be fulfilling and enjoyable.

So there's no "knead for loafing." Let's get going and bake some great breads!

Betty Crocker

P.S. Mmm. Can't you just taste your favorite jam slathered on a thick slice of warm fresh-baked bread.

Contents

Baking Bread with Love

Five Steps to Great Bread

A bread machine is easy to use after you become familiar with it. Here are five tips that will help make your bread baking a success in your kitchen.

1. KNOW YOUR BREAD MACHINE.

   Read your bread machine's use-and-care book carefully, especially the tips and hints. Understand how the machine's cycles work, and use them correctly. For example, do not reset the machine in the middle of a cycle. Although checking the dough while it's mixing is a good idea (see The Proof Is in the Dough on page 16), never open your machine during the rising or baking stages to check the progress because the rising loaf could collapse.

   *If your machine has delay cycles, choose them only for recipes that **do not** contain fresh fruits and vegetables, honey, meats, eggs or fresh dairy products (delay cycles can be used for recipes that include margarine or butter). If these ingredients stand in the machine for several hours, they can possibly cause bacteria growth and food poisoning. When using a delay cycle, be sure the yeast does not come in contact with liquid or wet ingredients.*

2. ASSEMBLE YOUR MACHINE CORRECTLY.

   Make sure the pan, blade and other parts are correctly assembled for proper mixing and kneading (see your bread machine's use-and-care book for complete details). If the bread machine parts are used incorrectly, the dough may not mix, knead, rise or bake properly. Be sure the blade, also called the paddle, is inserted correctly in the pan before adding the ingredients. If the blade is not inserted correctly, the bread will not knead properly.

3. READ AND UNDERSTAND YOUR RECIPE.

   Be sure to use only the ingredients called for, and measure them carefully because over- or undermeasuring can affect the results. Use standard household measuring cups and spoons. Measure dry ingredients and solid fats in graduated nested measuring cups. Glass measuring cups should be used for all liquids, including sticky liquids such as honey and molasses.

4. PREPARE INGREDIENTS BEFORE STARTING.

   Select fresh, high-quality ingredients, and use the types of ingredients generally recommended for bread machine baking.

   Assemble ingredients on your kitchen counter in the order they will be added to the bread pan. For best results, ingredients should be at room temperature, except for those ingredients normally stored in the refrigerator, such as fresh milk and eggs. If you store flour or grains in the refrigerator or freezer, be sure the measured ingredients come to room temperature before adding them to the bread pan. Check the recipe or follow the order recommended in your bread machine's use-and-care book to be sure that all the ingredients have been added in the correct order.

5. MAKE RECIPE CHANGES ONE AT A TIME.

   As you become familiar with your bread machine, you may get the urge to experiment by changing the ingredients of a bread machine recipe. Make just one change at a time, so you know what does or does not work. Check Let's Make a Great Bread

Machine Loaf on pages 14 and 15 to see what adjustments to make if the revised recipe didn't give you the quality loaf you want.

Basic Cycle Features

Cycles, also called settings or modes, really enhance the versatility of bread machines. Although all machines offer the basic white and whole wheat bread cycles, many machines are equipped with special cycles. To help you out, we've included some key features so you can check out at a glance the features on your bread machine. We do recommend, however, that you read the use-and-care book that came with your machine, so you fully understand how to use your bread machine.

Basic bread cycles are cycles that let you choose your favorite crust color for most bread recipes, including rye and white breads. The crust colors are medium (regular), dark or light. During these cycles, the bread machine will knead the dough twice, rise the dough twice, shape it and then bake it. Most breads will be best at medium setting but some that are higher in sugar might be better at a light setting. If you like a thicker, darker crust, then dark is the setting you will want to use. Using the setting that your recipe specifies is best, then change it the next time you make the recipe if you want a different crust.

Whole wheat or *whole-grain cycle* is a setting for recipes that have significant amounts of whole wheat or rye flour, oats or bran. It has a longer rising and preheat time to allow heavier grains to expand. Generally, these loaves will be shorter and denser than basic breads.

Dough cycle is a useful feature if you want to use your machine for making dough for pizza, coffee cakes, rolls or other shaped breads. This program does not bake, nor does it have a keep-warm function. The dough is kneaded twice and allowed to rise once in the machine. Then you can remove the dough, shape it by hand, let it rise and bake it in your regular oven.

French or crisp cycle will give you a bread with a crusty exterior and soft inside texture. During this cycle, the bread machine will knead the dough twice, rise the dough twice, shape it and bake it to perfection.

Sweet or sweet bread cycle is used for making breads with cheese or a high sugar or fat content. The result is a bread with a golden brown crust and a dense, moist inside texture. With this cycle, the baking temperature is usually lower so the outside of the bread won't burn. The bread machine will knead the dough twice, rise the dough twice, shape it and then bake it. This setting requires a little more resting and shaping time, so if fruits or nuts were added at the raisin/nut signal, they will have time to settle in the dough.

Raisin/Nut signal lets you know with a beeping sound when to add fruit or nuts to the dough. The signal beeps about 5 minutes before the end of the kneading cycle. This helps to retain the shape and texture of the ingredient.

Rapid or rapid-bake cycle cuts the knead and rise times. Usually, the loaf is ready about an hour sooner than with the basic cycle. Keep in mind that the use of the word "rapid" is relative; rapid cycles on some machines are actually longer than the regular cycle on others.

Quick cycle is a cycle for making no-yeast breads. These breads use baking powder for the leavening instead of yeast. The cycle is faster and will mix the ingredients and bake the loaf.

Delay, delayed-bake, delay-start or timed bake lets you program the machine to start at a later time, for some bread machines up to sixteen hours later! This feature is great to have if you want to wake up to or come home to freshly baked bread. **DO NOT USE THIS CYCLE IF YOUR RECIPE HAS FRESH MEATS, EGGS, HONEY, FRUITS, VEGETABLES OR FRESH DAIRY PRODUCTS SUCH AS MILK, CHEESE, SOUR CREAM, CREAM CHEESE OR YOGURT.** Bacteria could grow while these ingredients stand in the machine for several hours. You can substitute dry milk and water for fresh milk and use the delay cycle if no other perishable ingredients listed on page 7 are in a recipe. When using the delay cycle, be sure the yeast does not come in contact with liquids, wet ingredients or salt or else it will be activated too soon and won't work when it needs to make the bread rise.

Most bread machines feature several of the cycles we have mentioned above. Here are some additional features you may want to consider for your next bread machine purchase.

Take a peek! Some machines include a *viewing window* on top so you can watch the bread as it is mixed, kneaded and baked.

A *bucket-style pan* comes in handy if your ingredients aren't near your bread machine. The pan is removable, so you can load the ingredients on the counter or in the machine.

Some machines have a separate compartment that adds yeast after the other ingredients are mixed. Although a *yeast dispenser* is a common feature on many machines, it's not necessary. It's just as easy to dump all of the dry ingredients, including the yeast, into the machine at the same time.

A *keep-warm* or *cool-down* feature helps keep the bread from "sweating" in the pan or getting too moist from the moisture in the closed bread machine after it has been baked. You'll appreciate the dual advantages of this feature—the crust stays crisp and the bread stays warm for at least an hour after it bakes.

A *power-outage protection* feature continues bread processing if you experience a brief interruption in power.

When it's time to clean up, you'll want a bread pan and dough blade with *nonstick coating*. A quick and easy cleaning with a sponge and hot, soapy water is all it takes to clean the pan and blade.

Some machines also have settings for making jam, jelly, pasta dough, cake, fudge, pudding, rice and yogurt. Some even roast meats! Of course, it is your decision if you need these capabilities on your bread machine.

Know Your Bread Ingredients

All that is needed to make bread is flour, water, yeast and sometimes a little salt. Many of us also like sweeter and richer breads and coffee cakes, so we add sugar, fat, milk and eggs to those basic ingredients. Read on to familiarize yourself with the roles of the different ingredients used to make bread.

Flour

Flour is the primary ingredient, by amount, in bread making. When wheat flour is mixed with liquid and then kneaded, the proteins in the flour go together and form sheets of gluten. Gluten is important because it allows the dough to stretch like elastic, trapping the bubbles of gas given off by the yeast.

Other grains—including corn, rye, barley, rice and millet, to name a few—can be ground into flour. They don't have enough protein to make the gluten necessary for the dough to rise. However, these grain flours can be mixed with wheat flour to make yeast doughs. We recommend using at least half wheat flour and half of a low- or no-gluten-producing flour. Check Flour Power! on pages 10 and 11 to learn more about flour.

Measuring Flour

All flour is sifted many times during the milling process and some flours are labeled "presifted." If a recipe calls for sifted flour but you do not want to sift it, there is no need to adjust the amount of flour in the recipe. To obtain the most accurate measurement of flour, spoon flour into a standard dry-ingredient measuring cup and level the top with a knife or spatula.

Storing Flour

Store all flours in airtight canisters in a cool, dry place. Use all-purpose flour, unbleached flour, and bread flour within fifteen months, self-rising flour within nine months and whole wheat and wheat-blend flours within six to eight months. If flour is to be kept for an extended period of time, store it in a moisture-proof bag in the refrigerator or freezer. Allow flour to come to room temperature before using it.

Humidity and Flour

Because flour picks up and loses moisture over a period of time, humidity will affect the use of flour in recipes. When making a recipe, you may need to use less or more flour, but do not change the liquid measurement in the recipe. Gradually add more flour as needed, a tablespoon at a time, if the dough is too wet, or add a little more liquid, a teaspoon at a time, if it is too dry. Check The Proof Is in the Dough on page 16 to see how your dough should look.

Yeast

Yeast is a leavening agent that is made up of thousands of tiny living plants. When given moisture, warmth and "food," yeast will grow and release tiny bubbles of carbon dioxide gas; this process makes dough rise. Yeast is very sensitive; too much heat will kill it, and cold will stunt its growth. Always check the expiration date of the yeast you are using. Basically, three forms of yeast are readily available in supermarkets for home baking.

Bread machine and quick active dry yeast are highly active strains of dry yeast that make dough rise faster than regular active dry yeast. Bread machine yeast was introduced in 1993. It is a special strain of instant yeast, packaged in jars, to end consumer confusion about what kind of yeast works best in bread machines. Because of its finer granulation, the yeast is dispersed more thoroughly during mixing and kneading. Quick active dry yeast can be purchased in premeasured packets and in jars.

Regular active dry yeast is yeast that has been dried and then packaged in a granular form. It can be purchased in premeasured packets and in jars.

These three types of dry yeast are generally interchangeable, although adjustments sometimes are required. We recommend using bread machine yeast or quick active dry yeast in the recipes in this cookbook. If you find that bread machine or quick active dry yeast makes bread rise too high for your bread machine, decrease the amount by 1/4 teaspoon at a time when you make the recipe again.

Compressed cake or fresh active yeast is also available in cake form. Generally, fresh yeast is not used in bread machines because measuring it accurately is difficult.

If You Don't Have Bread Machine Yeast. . .

Here is how much regular active dry yeast you should use instead.

Bread Machine or Quick Active Dry Yeast	Regular Active Dry Yeast
3/4 teaspoon	1 teaspoon
1 teaspoon	1 1/2 teaspoons
1 1/2 teaspoons	2 teaspoons

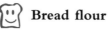 = *Great for Breads*   = *Not So Great for Breads*

We have included descriptions of flours and flour-blends here, so you will know which flour to use if you want to experiment with your bread machine.

All-purpose flour   A blend of hard wheats and soft wheats, making it suitable for all types of baking. Bleaching agents are used in small amounts to whiten the flour and improve baking results. All-purpose flour can be used when baking bread, but you will get better results with bread flour in the bread machine.

Bread flour   An unbleached flour made from a special blend of hard wheats, which are higher in protein. It contains small amounts of malted barley flour, which feeds the yeast, and potassium bromate to increase the elasticity of the gluten. Bread flour absorbs a greater quantity of water and produces a more elastic dough, resulting in tall, well-formed loaves. It is the ideal flour to use in bread machines because it is high in gluten-forming proteins.

Cake flour   Cake flour is milled from soft wheat to produce a flour that is low in gluten-forming protein. It is excellent for baking biscuits, pastries and fine-textured cakes, but it doesn't have enough gluten to make good bread.

Organic flour   Organic flour does not contain the bleaches, bromates or other additives that are sometimes found in all-purpose flour. The word "organic" usually means that the wheat has been grown using only natural fertilizers and that it has not been sprayed with pesticides. Organic certification varies from state to state, but the wheat must be tested and must pass the certification process before it can be labeled organic. Organic flour can be used in bread machine recipes.

Quick-mixing flour   This is a unique instantized all-purpose flour. It is granular in texture, pours freely and is dust free. Because it dissolves instantly in cold liquids, it is excellent for making smooth sauces, gravies and batters. We do not recommend using quick-mix flours for bread machine recipes because it sometimes absorbs more liquid than other flours do.

= Great for Breads   = Not So Great for Breads

Rye flour

Rye flour is milled from rye grain and is low in gluten-forming protein. It is usually combined with wheat flour to increase the gluten-forming capabilities of the dough when used in bread machines for baking bread.

Self-rising flour

An all-purpose flour with the leavening and salt added. It produces high, light biscuits and tender, fine-textured cakes. Self-rising flour isn't for bread machine recipes because of the added leavening.

Semolina flour

A golden, grainy flour made from durum wheat. Durum wheat is a hard winter wheat that contains high-gluten proteins, but it isn't a good baking flour. Instead, it is excellent for making pasta.

Stone-ground whole wheat flour

This flour is coarser than roller-milled whole wheat flour. Breads made with whole wheat flour have a nutty flavor and dense texture. Because whole wheat flour has less protein, whole wheat breads do not rise as high as breads made with bread flour or all-purpose flour. For better volume, use half whole wheat flour with half bread flour or all-purpose flour.

Unbleached flour

An all-purpose flour that has no bleaching agents added. It is not as white as all-purpose flour, so baked products will have more of a creamy color. Unbleached flour can be used for baking bread, but you will get better results with bread flour.

Whole wheat flour

This is made with the complete wheat kernel, so it contains the bran, germ and endosperm. It is best to store whole wheat flour in the freezer or refrigerator to help prevent the germ from becoming rancid. Be sure to allow the measured amount of flour for your recipe to come to room temperature before adding it to the other ingredients.

Wheat-blend bread flour

A special flour blend that produces wheat loaves higher in volume and lighter in taste and texture than those made with 100 percent whole wheat flour. Wheat-blend bread flour can be substituted cup for cup in recipes that call for all-purpose, whole wheat or bread flour.

Sweeteners

Sweeteners, including sugar, honey and molasses, provide food for the yeast to grow. They also add flavor and help the crust to brown. Sweeteners vary in flavor intensity and dissolving rate, so it is important to use the sweetener called for in the recipe.

Some ingredients such as fruits and some vegetables contain natural sugars. Too much sugar may interfere with the development of the gluten, and the baked product could collapse. Too much sugar also can inhibit the growth of the yeast. So if you are adding fruits or vegetables to your favorite white bread, you may have to increase the amount of yeast. We don't recommend using artificial sweeteners because they do not properly "feed" the yeast.

Salt

Salt enhances the flavor of bread and strengthens the dough by tightening and improving the gluten. It also controls yeast growth, so the flavors have time to develop. Too much salt, however, can kill the yeast, so it is important to measure accurately. Salt also acts as a preservative, which helps keep the bread fresher longer. A salt-free loaf will be high and light with a coarser texture, but it will lack in flavor.

We use table salt for our recipe testing because it is a staple in most homes. Coarse or kosher salt is not used in the recipes but sometimes is used for sprinkling on top of bread doughs before baking, since it adds both flavor and a nice appearance to baked breads. We don't recommend using reduced- or low-sodium salt because it results in a poorer-quality baked product.

Fats and Oils

Fats, such as shortening, margarine, butter and oil tenderize baked goods, help bind ingredients together, aid in browning and add richness and flavor to yeast doughs.

Not all fats are created equal in texture, flavor or baking characteristics. If using a vegetable-oil spread, be sure it contains at least 65 percent fat. We do not recommend using whipped or tub products in the bread machine. Due to added air or liquid, the whipped, tub and low-fat vegetable-oil spreads are not recommended for baking bread because the results are not satisfactory.

Liquids

Liquid is used to rehydrate and activate the yeast and to blend with the flour to make a soft, elastic dough. Water and milk are the most commonly used liquids. Water gives bread a crisper crust, and milk gives bread a velvety texture and added nutrients. Buttermilk or sour milk can be substituted for fresh milk if you like a tangy flavor. Do not use delay cycles with recipes that contain fresh milk because the milk can spoil and possibly cause bacteria growth and food poisoning.

Dry milk (in its dry form) often is used in bread machine recipes so that the delay cycles can be used. Only the recipes that use dry milk and have no perishable ingredients, such as meats, eggs, dairy products or honey, can be used with the delay cycles. Dry buttermilk can be substituted for dry milk in recipes. If dry milk is not available, fresh milk can be substituted for the amount of water and dry milk called for in the recipe, but remember not to use the delay cycles.

Other than water and milk, room-temperature beer, wine and fruit and vegetables juices can also be used in bread making. And that's not the only source of liquid! Any ingredient that becomes soft or melts in the dough will add liquid, including cheese, sour cream, cream cheese and yogurt. Ingredients such as fresh fruits and vegetables also can add liquid to doughs. Ingredients that have been soaked before being added to the dough will add liquid, including raisins, dried fruit or dried mushrooms.

Eggs

Eggs are added to bread doughs for taste, richness and color. They also act as emulsifiers and will slow the staling process and help keep bread stay fresh a little longer. Do not use delay cycles with recipes that contain eggs because the eggs can spoil and possibly cause bacteria growth and food poisoning.

Egg washes can be made with beaten egg, egg whites or a mixture of water and egg. This is brushed on the shaped dough before baking to give bread a beautiful golden brown crust.

High-Altitude

High-altitude areas (areas that are 3,500 feet or higher above sea level) will require some changes in the bread machine recipe. Air pressure is lower, so the bread will rise higher. Start by reducing the amount of yeast by 1/4 teaspoon; if the loaf is still too high, reduce the yeast more the next time.

Flour dries out more quickly at high altitude, so check the dough during the kneading cycle to be sure it isn't too dry. Add water, about a teaspoon at a time, until the dough forms a smooth ball. You may want to check The Proof Is in the Dough on pages 16 and 17 to see how the dough should look during the kneading cycle.

Check your bread machine's use-and-care book for more high-altitude adjustments, or call your local United States Department of Agriculture (USDA) Extension Service office. You will find the Extension Service office listed in the phone book under "County Government."

Measuring Your Bread Machine Pan Size

The size of a bread pan is determined by how much water the pan holds. Plug the opening in the bottom of the pan with a crumpled piece of aluminum foil. Measure water in a standard liquid-ingredient measuring cup. Pour the water into the bread pan until it is full, keeping track of many cups it took to fill it. You may want to note the amount of water in your bread machine use-and-care book so you have it next time you need to know the size of the pan.

Loaf Size	Amount of Flour	Minimum Pan Capacity
1-pound	2 cups	8 cups
1 1/2-pound	3 cups	10 cups
2-pound	4 cups	13 cups

Let's Make a Great Bread Machine Loaf

What is a great loaf of bread? It if tastes good and looks good, that's everything! Your bread machine occasionally may produce a loaf that does not meet your expectations. Each bread machine works a little differently, so you may need to make slight ingredient changes to the recipe so it works in your machine. Remember that correctly measuring all ingredients carefully is the first important step to a good loaf of bread.

If the Loaf Is	*This Could Be the Reason*
Short, unsatisfactory rising	• Not enough sugar. • Not enough yeast, or the yeast was old or improperly stored. • Delay timer was used and ingredients were placed in bread pan so that the salt or water were in contact with the yeast for a long period. • Short, heavier loaves are to be expected when using whole grains or whole-grain flours or when using all-purpose flour instead of bread flour. Try using bread flour and reducing the amount of other flours and grains. • The bread pan was too large for the recipe loaf size.
No rise 	• Yeast was old or improperly stored, or yeast was forgotten or mismeasured. • Other key ingredients were forgotten or mismeasured. • Delay timer was used and ingredients were placed in the pan incorrectly.
Collapsed	• Ingredient amounts were out of proportion. • Salt was omitted. • The bread pan was too small for the amount of dough. • The dough rose to the top of the machine and interfered with circulation needed for proper baking and cooling. • Warm weather, high humidity or overheated liquids all speed up yeast action, which may cause the dough to rise too fast and the bread to collapse before baking begins. To help avoid this, bake during the coolest part of the day, avoid delay cycles and use refrigerated liquids. • Bread machine was opened during rising and baking cycles. • The baked loaf was left in the bread machine too long.

If you encounter a problem with your bread machine bread, try only one change at a time, rather than trying several changes at once. For example, if the loaf has a mushroom-shaped top, there could be three different reasons why that happened. One reason could be too much yeast. The next time you make the recipe, decrease the yeast by 1/4 teaspoon, and jot down the results.

If the Loaf Is	This Could Be the Reason
Mushroom-shaped top 	• Usually indicates that ingredient quantities were out of proportion. Too much yeast, sugar, flour, liquid or a combination may result in the dough exceeding the capacity of the pan. • Bread pan was too small for the amount of dough. • Too many sugary ingredients were used. Reduce the amount by 1 tablespoon.
Gummy layer 	• Too much whole-grain flour or whole grains. • Too much wet or rich ingredients such as applesauce, eggs, etc. • Bread pan was too small for the amount of dough, so the loaf is underbaked.
Open, coarse or holey texture 	• Too much water was used. • Too much yeast was used, or yeast action was accelerated by hot humid weather or overheated ingredients. • Salt was omitted. • Drain fruit and vegetables well and pat dry before adding to bread pan.
Heavy, dense texture 	• Not enough water was used. • Not enough sugar was used. • Not enough yeast was used. • Too much flour was used. • Be sure salt was added. • Too much whole-grain flour or whole grains were used. Substitute half bread flour. • The proportion of ingredients was imbalanced by too much dried fruits or other added ingredients.

Here's How We Test the Recipes

Each recipe has been carefully tested with a variety of bread machines.

Bread flour was used for all our recipes and sometimes combined with other flour, such as whole wheat or rye. We use bread flour because it is high in protein, which is necessary for successful bread baking.

Bread machine yeast was used for testing all the recipes. We found that quick active dry yeast should not require any adjustments. However, if you use regular active dry yeast, you may need to increase yeast by 1/4 to 1/2 teaspoon per loaf.

Many recipes include directions for making both 1 1/2-pound and 2-pound loaves. There is also a special chapter for making 1-pound loaves, for those times when a smaller loaf is what you need. Loaf size is determined by the size of your bread machine pan. Check your bread machine's use-and-care book to find out what size loaf your bread machine makes, or use the following guidelines to determine what size recipe you should use.

We found that yeast amounts vary among the different sizes of loaves and different types of bread. Some recipes for 2-pound loaves actually call for less yeast than the 1 1/2-pound recipe. If you are uncertain about how the bread will perform in your machine, try the recipe as written. If you would like a 2-pound loaf with more height—and your bread machine pan can hold it—increase the yeast by 1/4 teaspoon.

We use table salt for our recipe testing because it is a staple in most homes. Coarse or kosher salt is not used in the recipes but sometimes is used for sprinkling on top of bread doughs before baking, since it adds both flavor and a nice appearance to baked breads. We don't recommend using reduced- or low-sodium salt because it results in a poorer-quality baked product.

We used low-fat milk for our testing, but you can use whole, skim or nonfat milk.

We used large eggs when testing our recipes.

We do not recommend making the bread machine loaves in glass-domed bread machines. Our results were inconsistent, and the loaves were not satisfactory. However, the dough recipes work nicely in the glass-domed bread machines.

The height and shape of bread loaves may vary from one loaf to another depending on the humidity and room temperature. On a humid day, you may find you'll need to add a little more flour. Check The Proof Is in the Dough below to see if your dough is too moist during the kneading cycle.

The Proof Is in the Dough

Some things are out of our control when making dough. Many factors, including the weather, humidity and amount of moisture in the flour, affect the amount of flour necessary to make a smooth dough. To check your dough, you'll need to peek into the bread machine after the first three to five minutes of the kneading cycle.

Dough with the correct amount of flour and liquid will be soft, satiny and pliable. It will form a smooth ball of dough during kneading. During the rest cycle, the ball of dough will relax and spread to the corners of the pan.

If the dough looks dry and crumbly and the machine seems to be having difficulty kneading it, the dough needs more liquid. With the machine running, add liquid, about 1 teaspoon at a time, until the dough is smooth and forms a ball.

Wet, soggy dough that spreads to the sides of the pan and doesn't form a ball needs more flour. With the machine running, add bread flour, about 1 tablespoon at a time, until the dough is smooth and forms a ball.

Refrigerating Dough

One of the joys of the bread machine is you can easily make a dough and keep it in the refrigerator until you want to bake it. Doughs without egg will keep up to 48 hours in the refrigerator and doughs with egg should be stored no more than 24 hours.

Remove the dough from the bread machine pan, and shape it into a ball. Place it in a bowl greased with shortening or nonstick cooking spray. Grease or spray the top of the dough, and cover with plastic wrap and then with a damp cloth. Place the bowl in the refrigerator. When you are ready to bake the dough, shape it and let it rise, covered, in a warm place about 1 1/2 to 2 hours or until double. Bake the dough as the recipe instructs.

You also can shape the dough before refrigerating it. Look for the Do-Ahead Note with many of our dough recipes.

As to freezing dough, we like to follow "bake first, then freeze" for better-quality baked goods. Doughs can lose some of their rising power after freezing.

Betty's Tips for Shaping Dough

- "Lightly floured surface" means a cutting board or countertop over which 1 to 2 tablespoons of flour have been evenly sprinkled.
- "Greased bowl" means a bowl in which about 1 tablespoon shortening, margarine, butter or oil has been spread over the inside. Be sure the bowl is large enough so the dough can double in size.
- Let the dough rise as the recipe directs for the best texture and shaped bread. The recipe may say "until double" or "until almost double" in size.
- A great place for letting dough rise is an empty oven with a bowl of warm water placed at the bottom. Cover the dough with a lint-free towel or with plastic wrap. Remember to remove the dough before heating the oven for baking! Another draft-free place is your microwave. Place a bowl or measuring cup of hot water in the oven with the dough for added moisture.
- If the dough is soft and sticky, lightly dust your hands with flour before shaping the dough.
- When shaping dough, be sure your hands are free of soap or lotion, which could affect the taste and texture of the baked product.
- If you are rolling out dough, and it continues to "shrink back," cover it and let it rest for a few minutes and then try rolling again.

Keeping Bread Fresh

Homemade bread is best eaten the same day it is baked, but it will keep two or three days at room temperature.

Store bread at room temperature in a cool, dry place. Wrap the completely cooled bread in a tightly sealed paper bag if you plan to eat it within a day or two. Plastic bags keep the bread fresh but also promote molding. You might want to switch from paper to a plastic bag if there is any bread left after 2 days because the bread will be a little drier.

Breads keep best at room temperature or for longer periods of time in the freezer, rather than in the refrigerator. The only time you may want to store the bread in the refrigerator is during hot, humid weather to help prevent mold from forming.

Freezing Bread

To freeze a loaf of bread, seal the completely cooled loaf in an airtight plastic bag or wrap for freezing. You may want to slice the bread first to save thawing time later. Also, slicing makes it easy to remove just the number of slices you need at a time. You can freeze bread up to two to three months.

To thaw the bread, loosen the wrap and let it stand at room temperature about three hours. If you completely unwrap it before thawing, moisture collects and can make the bread soggy. Or to thaw a frozen bread machine loaf in the oven, wrap the loaf in aluminum foil and heat in 400° oven for 10 to 15 minutes or until thawed and warm.

Frozen bread slices can be thawed in the microwave. Heat each slice on High for about 15 seconds. Or pop frozen slices right into the toaster to thaw and toast in one easy step.

Coffee cakes, breadsticks and rolls also can be frozen after being cooled completely. We recommend not frosting or decorating before freezing. If you prefer to frost before freezing, be sure the frosting is dry and that a thin crust has formed so the frosting doesn't smear when being wrapped for the freezer. Seal tightly in an airtight plastic bag or wrap for freezing. You may want to slice coffee cakes before freezing so you can remove the number of slices you need, and slices will thaw more quickly. These breads will keep in the freezer for two to three months.

To thaw coffee cakes, breadsticks and rolls, let them stand loosely wrapped at room temperature two to three hours. After they have thawed, allow any moisture that may have collected on the surface to dry. Then frost or decorate as you wish.

Any Way You Want to Slice It

A long, scalloped-edge serrated bread knife or sharp straight-edge knife works great for cutting bread. Cut with a back-and-forth sawing motion. However, when cutting a warm bread loaf, we find that an electric knife works best. After cutting, place the loaf cut side down on a surface to help prevent it from drying out.

Bread machine loaves come in various shapes and sizes. Here are several ways to cut them.

- For square slices, place the loaf on its side and cut down through the loaf. We find this the easiest way to cut loaves.

- For rectangular slices, place the loaf upright and cut from the top down. Slices may be cut in half, either lengthwise or crosswise.

- For wedges, place the loaf upright and cut down from the center into wedges. Or cut the loaf in half from the top down, then place each half cut side down and cut lengthwise into wedges.

- For other shapes, use your imagination! Bread slices can be cut into triangles, fingerlike strips and chunks. Or slices can be cut with cookie cutters into other interesting and fun shapes.

Some Like It Hot: Reheating Your Bread

It is always a treat when warm bread is served at a meal. You can freshen up room-temperature bread machine loaves by heating them in the oven.

For a crisper crust, place the loaf right on the oven rack. Heat it in a 300° oven about 20 minutes or until the crust is crisp and warm. For a softer crust, wrap the loaf in aluminum foil before popping into the oven. You also can heat coffee cakes in aluminum foil the same way and then frost and decorate.

Bread slices and rolls can be warmed in the microwave, but you must be very careful so they don't overheat and become tough or hard.

Breads heated in the microwave become dry and tough faster than bread heated in a conventional or toaster oven, so plan to eat them right away.

Your Bread Machine Baking Questions

Many of our consumers call, write or E-mail us with questions they have about using their bread machine. Here are some of their frequently asked questions. We hope the convenience of having the answers in our cookbook will be helpful to you.

Q *Why does the dough blade turn slowly and intermittently the first few minutes?*

A Most bread machines will slowly and intermittently mix ingredients the first 5 minutes of kneading. Then the blade will turn quickly and begin to knead dough into a smooth ball. If after the first 5 minutes the dough blade doesn't turn quickly, the dough is too dry. Add liquid, about a tablespoon at a time, until the blade turns quickly.

Q *Why doesn't my bread machine bake the bread?*

A The Dough program was accidentally selected. Be sure to select the correct program for making bread.

Q *Why is my loaf of baked bread soggy after I remove it from my bread machine?*

A The hot loaf of bread was not removed from the pan after being baked. The bread will steam, which will cause the bread to be soft and soggy rather than crisp and dry on the outside. To prevent this from happening, remove the loaf from the machine as soon as it is done baking.

Also, warm weather, high humidity or overheated liquids all speed up yeast action, which may cause the dough to rise too fast and then collapse when the baking cycle begins. You can try using refrigerated liquids if your room temperature is over 80°. Also, do not use delay cycles. You can try reducing the yeast by 1/4 teaspoon during hot, humid weather.

Q *Why does my bread machine seem to be mixing and baking bread improperly?*

A It could be that the kneading blade is not rotating smoothly. Be sure the kneading blade shaft is free of all crumbs and any baked-on dough. Also, be sure the bread machine is getting a steady supply of electricity. It is best not to have another heat-producing appliance operating from the same outlet.

Q *What is the difference between the first and second rising stages?*

A The first rising allows the dough to double in size. The dough is then "punched down" so that the gas that has formed can escape. The second rising also lets the dough rise until double in size. These two risings create a more tender, evenly textured bread.

Q *Where has the kneading blade gone?*

A It may have been baked into the bottom of the loaf of bread. Be sure to remove the blade from the loaf. After the loaf is cool, carefully remove the kneading blade using the bowl end of a plastic spoon or other plastic or wooden utensil. We recommend plastic or wood so you don't scratch the nonstick finish on the kneading blade. If you need to remove the kneading blade from a hot bread loaf, be sure to use oven mitts or wrap the loaf in a kitchen towel so you won't burn yourself.

Q *What do I do if the kneading blade is difficult to remove from the pan after baking bread?*

A Fill the pan with hot water and wait a few minutes. Pour out the water, and the blade should be easy to remove. Be sure to wash all the baked-on bread off the kneading blade and the mounting shaft inside the pan to make the kneading blade easier to remove.

Q *Why don't the baked loaves always fill up the pan?*

A Not all bread recipes will fill the bread pan, but they still will have good texture and eating quality. Some breads are naturally more dense with lower volume due to whole-grain flour and other added ingredients such as nuts, fruits and cooked grains. If your loaves are low in volume but also too dense to be good eating quality, check Let's Make a Great Bread Machine Loaf on pages 14 and 15 to determine what might be causing the problem.

Q *What can I do when the bread sticks to the pan and won't come out?*

A Rap the pan on a cutting board to loosen the loaf, and it should slide out. Don't use a knife or metal spatula to loosen the loaf because it could scratch the nonstick finish inside the pan. We also recommend washing the pan by hand rather than in the dishwasher so the finish won't be damaged.

Q *When making a dough recipe, what do you mean when you say to cover?*

A You cover the dough to keep it from getting cold or from being in a draft while it is rising. Covering the dough also prevents a thin crust from forming on the surface of the shaped bread. When rising the dough before shaping, shape the dough into a ball. Place the ball of dough into a greased bowl that is large enough for the dough to double in size. Grease the top of the dough with oil, shortening, margarine or butter. Cover it with a lint-free kitchen towel. Or you can cover the bowl with plastic wrap. To cover the shaped dough, grease a piece of waxed paper, parchment paper or plastic wrap, and place it, greased side down, on the dough. Cover with a lint-free kitchen towel.

Q *What do you mean by a warm, draft-free place to let dough rise?*

A Dough needs to be away from drafts and have a warm, not hot, environment in which to rise properly. Covering the dough will keep drafts directly off the dough and help to keep it warm. The oven or microwave is a good draft-free choice. Some people use a cupboard, closet shelf or even the top of a clothes dryer. Look around your kitchen to find a good spot that works for you.

Q *When baking bread in my oven, how do I know when it is done?*

A Just because the bread is baked to a beautiful golden brown doesn't mean it is baked completely through. Tap the top of the bread, and then, using pot holders or kitchen towel, gently turn the bread over and tap the bottom; it should sound hollow. If it doesn't sound hollow or you want a darker crust, return the bread to the oven for a few more minutes. If you are baking a loaf of bread, you can return the loaf to the oven by placing it directly on the oven rack.

Q *Can I use all-purpose flour for my bread machine recipes?*

A While all of these recipes have been tested with bread flour, you may use all-purpose flour in your bread machine recipes. However, the volume will be lower and the texture will be slightly different than bread made with bread flour. Bread flour gives your loaf a better structure due to the higher gluten, so bread made with all-purpose flour isn't as tolerant to additional ingredients such as fruits, grains or vegetables.

Q *Can I use self-rising flour in my bread machine?*

A No, because the chemical leavening in self-rising flour will interfere with the yeast, and the result will not be satisfactory.

Q *How does warm, humid weather affect bread baked in a bread machine?*

A Flour absorbs and loses moisture over time. That is why it is important to store flour in an airtight container. Humidity can affect the amount of flour needed in your recipe. A humid climate may require a slightly higher amount of flour because the flour itself has absorbed moisture. In humid weather, try adding an extra tablespoon of flour for each cup of flour called for in the recipe. In areas of low humidity, try removing a tablespoon of flour from each cup of flour.

Q *How do I know if my jar of yeast is still good?*

A A method called "proofing the yeast" will determine if your yeast is still active. Fill a 1-cup glass-measuring cup with 1/2 cup warm water (between 110° and 115°). Add 1 teaspoon sugar, and stir until the sugar dissolves. Add 2 1/4 teaspoons yeast, and stir. Let it stand for 10 minutes at room temperature to allow it to ferment. After 10 minutes, a layer of foam should develop. If there is no or very little foam the yeast is no longer active. You will need to discard the remaining yeast and buy fresh yeast for your baking.

Good and Savory Loaves

Cheesy Mustard Pretzel Bread (page 41)

Classic White Bread

SUCCESS TIP

We found from our testing that for good texture and volume, slightly less yeast is needed in the 2-pound loaf than is needed in the 1 1/2-pound loaf.

SUCCESS TIP

Who doesn't like a good slice of homemade bread? This loaf may become a family favorite because it is perfect to use the delay cycle with—which means you can have fresh bread whenever you like.

SANDWICH BOARD

This Grilled Pesto Mozzarella made with homemade white bread will make your next grilled cheese sandwich extra special. Butter the outside of the bread slices. Spread the inside of the bread with your favorite prepared pesto, and top with a few slices of mozzarella cheese. Layer with slices of fresh tomatoes, and sprinkle with fresh ground pepper if you like. Cover the tomatoes with more mozzarella cheese slices, and top with another slice of bread spread with pesto, then cook over medium heat until it's golden brown and the cheese is melted.

1 1/2-Pound Recipe (12 slices)		2-Pound Recipe (16 slices)
1 cup plus 2 tablespoons	Water	1 1/2 cups
2 tablespoons	Margarine or butter, softened	2 tablespoons
3 cups	Bread flour	4 cups
3 tablespoons	Dry milk	3 tablespoons
2 tablespoons	Sugar	2 tablespoons
1 1/2 teaspoons	Salt	2 teaspoons
2 teaspoons	Bread machine or quick active dry yeast	1 1/2 teaspoons

Make 1 1/2-Pound Recipe with bread machines that use 3 cups flour, or make 2-Pound Recipe with bread machines that use 4 cups flour.

Measure carefully, placing all ingredients in bread machine pan in the order recommended by the manufacturer.

Select Basic/White cycle. Use Medium or Light crust color. Remove baked bread from pan, and cool on wire rack.

◼ 1 Slice: 145 calories (20 calories from fat); 2g fat (0g saturated); 0mg cholesterol; 300mg sodium; 29g carbohydrate (1g dietary fiber); 4g protein

Sally Lunn

1 1/2-Pound Recipe (12 slices)		2-Pound Recipe (16 slices)
1 egg plus enough water to equal 1 cup plus 2 tablespoons	Egg(s)	2 eggs plus enough water to equal 1 1/3 cups
1 teaspoon	Salt	1 1/2 teaspoons
1 tablespoon plus 1 teaspoon	Sugar	2 tablespoons
1/4 cup plus 2 tablespoons	Butter, softened	1/3 cup
3 cups	Bread flour	4 cups
1 teaspoon	Bread machine or quick active dry yeast	1 1/2 teaspoons

Make 1 1/2-Pound Recipe with bread machines that use 3 cups flour, or make 2-Pound Recipe with bread machines that use 4 cups flour.

Measure carefully, placing all ingredients in bread machine pan in the order recommended by the manufacturer.

Select Basic/White cycle. Use Medium or Light crust color. Do not use delay cycles. Remove baked bread from pan, and cool on wire rack.

■ 1 Slice: 185 calories (65 calories from fat); 7g fat (4g saturated); 35mg cholesterol; 220mg sodium; 28g carbohydrate (1g dietary fiber); 4g protein

DID YOU KNOW?

Sally Lunn bread is believed to have been named after the Englishwoman who created this bread in her tiny bakery in Bath, England. The recipe was brought to the colonies and soon became a favorite in the South.

Sourdough Loaf

1 1/2-Pound Recipe (12 slices)		2-Pound Recipe (16 slices)
1 1/4 cups	Sourdough Starter (below)	1 1/2 cups
1/4 cup	Water	1/3 cup
3 cups	Bread flour	4 cups
1 tablespoon	Sugar	1 tablespoon
1 teaspoon	Salt	1 teaspoon
1 teaspoon	Bread machine yeast	1 1/4 teaspoons

Make 1 1/2-Pound Recipe with bread machines that use 3 cups flour, or make 2-Pound Recipe with bread machines that use 4 cups flour.

Remove Sourdough Starter from refrigerator at least 2 hours before starting bread. Measure correct amount for recipe, and let stand until room temperature. The starter will expand as it warms up. (Replenish remaining starter as directed in Sourdough Starter recipe.)

Measure carefully, placing all ingredients in bread machine pan in the order recommended by the manufacture.

Select Basic/White cycle. Use Medium or Light crust color. Remove baked bread from pan, and cool on wire rack.

■ 1 Slice: 175 calories (10 calories from fat); 1g fat (0g saturated); 0mg cholesterol; 210mg sodium; 37g carbohydrate (1g dietary fiber); 5g protein

Sourdough Starter

1 teaspoon bread machine or quick active dry yeast

1/4 cup warm water (105° to 115°)

3/4 cup milk

1 cup bread flour or all-purpose flour

Dissolve yeast in warm water in large glass bowl. Stir in milk. Gradually stir in flour. Beat until smooth. Cover with towel or cheesecloth; let stand in warm, draft-free place (80° to 85°) about 24 hours or until starter begins to ferment (bubbles will appear on surface of starter). If starter has not begun fermentation after 24 hours, discard and begin again.

Stir well, if fermentation has begun; cover tightly with plastic wrap and return to warm place. Let stand 2 to 3 days or until foamy. When starter has become foamy, stir well; pour into 1-quart crock or glass jar with tight-fitting cover. Store in refrigerator. When a clear liquid has risen to top, starter is ready to use. Stir before using.

Replenish remaining starter after removing starter for bread recipe. Add 3/4 cup milk and 3/4 cup flour. Store uncovered at room temperature about 12 hours or until bubbles appear. Cover and refrigerate.

Pumpkin Seed Bread

1 1/2-Pound Recipe (12 slices)		2-Pound Recipe (16 slices)
3/4 cup plus 2 tablespoons	Water	1 1/4 cups
1 1/2 teaspoons	Salt	2 teaspoons
2 tablespoons	Honey	3 tablespoons
2 tablespoons	Olive or vegetable oil	3 tablespoons
3 1/4 cups	Bread flour	4 1/2 cups
1/2 cup	Unsalted raw pumpkin seeds	3/4 cup
1 teaspoon	Bread machine or quick active dry yeast	1 teaspoon

Make 1 1/2-Pound Recipe with bread machines that use at least 3 cups flour, or make 2-Pound Recipe with bread machines that use at least 4 cups flour.

Measure carefully, placing all ingredients in bread machine pan in the order recommended by the manufacturer.

Select Sweet or Basic/White cycle. Use Medium or Light crust color. Do not use delay cycles. Remove baked bread from pan, and cool on wire rack.

■ 1 Slice: 190 calories (45 calories from fat); 5g fat (1g saturated); 0mg cholesterol; 270mg sodium; 32g carbohydrate (2g dietary fiber); 6g protein

SUCCESS TIP

We found from our testing that the same amount of yeast is needed for both the 1 1/2-pound and 2-pound loaves.

TRY THIS

If you prefer sunflower nuts, use unsalted raw ones instead of the pumpkin seeds.

DID YOU KNOW?

Pumpkin seeds are also known as *pepitas* (pronounced puh-PEE-tahs) and are a popular ingredient in Mexican cooking. After the white hull is removed, the medium-dark green seed is enjoyed for its delicate flavor. Look for pumpkin seeds in larger supermarkets or natural foods stores.

Mediterranean Herbed Bread

We found from our testing that the same amount of yeast is needed for both the 1 1/2-pound and 2-pound loaves.

Dried herbs can be used when fresh herbs aren't available. For the 1 1/2-pound loaf, use 1/2 teaspoon each of dried basil, oregano and thyme leaves; for the 2-pound loaf, use 3/4 teaspoon of each.

1 1/2-Pound Recipe (12 slices)		2-Pound Recipe (16 slices)
1 cup	Water	1 cup plus 3 tablespoons
1 tablespoon	Margarine or butter, softened	1 tablespoon
3 cups	Bread flour	4 cups
2 tablespoons	Sugar	2 tablespoons
1 tablespoon	Dry milk	1 tablespoon
1 1/2 teaspoons	Salt	1 3/4 teaspoons
1 teaspoon	Chopped fresh basil leaves	1 1/2 teaspoons
1 teaspoon	Chopped fresh oregano leaves	1 1/2 teaspoons
1 teaspoon	Chopped fresh thyme leaves	1 teaspoon
2 1/4 teaspoons	Bread machine or quick active dry yeast	2 1/4 teaspoons

Make 1 1/2-Pound Recipe with bread machines that use 3 cups flour, or make 2-Pound Recipe with bread machines that use 4 cups flour.

Measure carefully, placing all ingredients in bread machine pan in the order recommended by the manufacturer.

Select Basic/White cycle. Use Medium or Light crust color. Remove baked bread from pan, and cool on wire rack.

■ 1 Slice: 135 calories (10 calories from fat); 1g fat (0g saturated); 0mg cholesterol; 300mg sodium; 29g carbohydrate (1g dietary fiber); 4g protein

Mediterranean Herbed Bread

Beer Nut Bread

1 1/2-Pound Recipe (12 slices)		*2-Pound Recipe* (16 slices)
3/4 cup	Flat beer or nonalcoholic beer	1 cup
1/3 cup	Water	1/3 cup
3 tablespoons	Packed brown sugar	1/4 cup
1/2 cup	Shredded smoked Cheddar cheese	2/3 cup
1 tablespoon	Margarine or butter, softened	2 tablespoons
3 cups	Bread flour	4 cups
3/4 teaspoon	Salt	1 teaspoon
1 1/2 teaspoons	Bread machine or quick active dry yeast	1 3/4 teaspoons
1/2 cup	Salted peanuts	2/3 cup

Make 1 1/2-Pound Recipe with bread machines that use 3 cups flour, or make 2-Pound Recipe with bread machines that use 4 cups flour.

Measure carefully, placing all ingredients except peanuts in bread machine pan in the order recommended by the manufacturer. Add peanuts at the Raisin/Nut signal.

Select Basic/White cycle. Use Medium or Light crust color. Do not use delay cycles. Remove baked bread from pan, and cool on wire rack.

■ 1 Slice: 200 calories (55 calories from fat); 6g fat (2g saturated); 5mg cholesterol; 210mg sodium; 31g carbohydrate (1g dietary fiber); 6g protein

SUCCESS TIP

For flat beer, open the can or bottle and let it stand about 1 hour before using. The flat beer is necessary for a good-textured bread.

SUCCESS TIP

If your bread machine doesn't have a Raisin/Nut signal, add the peanuts 5 to 10 minutes before the last kneading cycle ends. Check your bread machine's use-and-care book to find out how long the last kneading cycle runs.

TRY THIS

The smoked Cheddar cheese adds a subtle smoky flavor, which goes nicely with the salted peanuts. Regular sharp or mild Cheddar cheese will also give you a loaf of tasty bread.

Herbed Vinaigrette Bread

1 1/2-Pound Recipe (12 slices)		2-Pound Recipe (16 slices)
3/4 cup plus 2 tablespoons	Water	1 cup plus 2 tablespoons
1 tablespoon	Balsamic vinegar	2 tablespoons
1/3 cup	Chopped red onion	1/2 cup
1 tablespoon	Vegetable oil	1 tablespoon
3 cups	Bread flour	4 cups
1 teaspoon	Dried tarragon leaves	1 1/2 teaspoons
2 tablespoons	Sugar	2 tablespoons
3/4 teaspoon	Salt	1 teaspoon
2 teaspoons	Bread machine or quick active dry yeast	2 teaspoons

Make 1 1/2–Pound Recipe with bread machines that use 3 cups flour, or make 2–Pound Recipe with bread machines that use 4 cups flour.

Measure carefully, placing all ingredients in bread machine pan in the order recommended by the manufacturer.

Select Basic/White cycle. Use Medium or Light crust color. Do not use delay cycles. Remove baked bread from pan, and cool on wire rack.

■ 1 Slice: 145 calories (20 calories from fat); 2g fat (0g saturated); 0mg cholesterol; 150mg sodium; 29g carbohydrate (1g dietary fiber); 4g protein

SUCCESS TIP

We found from our testing that the same amount of yeast is needed for both the 1 1/2-pound and 2-pound loaves.

TRY THIS

No balsamic vinegar in the pantry? You can substitute an apple cider vinegar or red wine vinegar instead.

DID YOU KNOW?

Balsamic (pronounced bal-SAH-mihk) vinegar is an exquisite Italian vinegar. It gets its rich deep color and slight sweetness from the wood barrel in which it is aged over a period of years.

Fiery Four-Pepper Bread

This fiery bread, "peppered" with four different forms of pepper, has a lower volume than other bread machine loaves. The texture and eating quality, however, is just as good as any taller loaf of bread.

Red pepper sauce is made from a very hot, small red pepper that originally came from the Mexican state of Tabasco. These peppers are now grown in parts of Louisiana. This fiery sauce is made from red pepper, vinegar and salt.

1 1/2-Pound Recipe (12 slices)		2-Pound Recipe (16 slices)
3/4 cup plus 3 tablespoons	Water	1 1/4 cups
1 tablespoon	Red pepper sauce	1 1/2 tablespoons
1 tablespoon	Chopped jalapeño chili	1 1/2 tablespoons
2 tablespoons	Margarine or butter, softened	2 tablespoons
3 cups	Bread flour	4 cups
1/4 teaspoon	Medium grind black pepper	1/2 teaspoon
1/2 teaspoon	Crushed red pepper	3/4 teaspoon
1 tablespoon	Sugar	2 tablespoons
1 teaspoon	Salt	1 1/4 teaspoons
1 1/2 teaspoons	Bread machine or quick active dry yeast	2 1/4 teaspoons

Make 1 1/2-Pound Recipe with bread machines that use 3 cups flour, or make 2-Pound Recipe with bread machines that use 4 cups flour.

Measure carefully, placing all ingredients in bread machine pan in the order recommended by the manufacturer.

Select Basic/White cycle. Use Medium or Light crust color. Do not use delay cycles. Remove baked bread from pan, and cool on wire rack.

■ 1 Slice: 140 calories (20 calories from fat); 2g fat (0g saturated); 0mg cholesterol; 230mg sodium; 28g carbohydrate (1g dietary fiber); 4g protein

Cheese Onion Bread

1 1/2-Pound Recipe (12 slices)		2-Pound Recipe (16 slices)
3/4 cup plus 2 tablespoons	Water	1 1/4 cups
3 cups	Bread flour	4 1/4 cups
3/4 cup	Shredded Cheddar cheese	1 cup
2 tablespoons	Sugar	1/4 cup
1 tablespoon	Dry milk	1 tablespoon
2 teaspoons	Instant minced onion	1 tablespoon
1 teaspoon	Salt	1 1/2 teaspoons
1 1/4 teaspoons	Bread machine or quick active dry yeast	1 1/2 teaspoons

Make 1 1/2-Pound Recipe with bread machines that use 3 cups flour, or make 2-Pound Recipe with bread machines that use at least 4 cups flour.

Measure carefully, placing all ingredients in bread machine pan in the order recommended by the manufacturer.

Select Basic/White cycle. Use Medium or Light crust color. Do not use delay cycles. Remove baked bread from pan, and cool on wire rack.

■ 1 Slice: 160 calories (25 calories from fat); 3g fat (2g saturated); 5mg cholesterol; 220mg sodium; 29g carbohydrate (1g dietary fiber); 5g protein

SUCCESS TIP

We don't recommend this recipe for bread machines that have cast-aluminum pans in a horizontal-loaf shape because our results after several tests were unsatisfactory.

SANDWICH BOARD

Friends dropping in later and you want a loaf of fresh homemade bread to serve? This is a great recipe to make since most of us have Cheddar cheese in the refrigerator and instant onion on the shelf to pop into the bread machine. Serve with slices of ham, a variety of mustards and a platter of fresh fruits for a tasty, welcoming lunch.

Roasted Garlic Bread

SUCCESS TIP

To be sure you will have enough roasted garlic, use at least a 2-ounce bulb of garlic for 2 tablespoons of roasted garlic and at least a 1-ounce bulb for 1 tablespoon.

SUCCESS TIP

If your bread machine doesn't have a Raisin/Nut signal, add the mashed garlic 5 to 10 minutes before the last kneading cycle ends. Check your bread machine's use-and-care book to find out how long the last cycle runs.

1 1/2-Pound Recipe (12 slices)		2-Pound Recipe (16 slices)
2 tablespoons mashed	Roasted Garlic (below)	3 tablespoons mashed
1 cup plus 2 tablespoons	Water	1 1/2 cups
1 tablespoon	Olive or vegetable oil	1 tablespoon
3 cups	Bread flour	4 cups
2 tablespoons	Sugar	2 tablespoons
1 teaspoon	Salt	1 teaspoon
1 1/4 teaspoons	Bread machine or quick active dry yeast	1 1/2 teaspoons

Make 1 1/2-Pound Recipe with bread machines that use 3 cups flour, or make 2-Pound Recipe with bread machines that use 4 cups flour.

Prepare Roasted Garlic. After squeezing garlic out of cloves, slightly mash enough garlic to measure 2 or 3 tablespoons.

Measure carefully, placing all ingredients except garlic in bread machine pan in the order recommended by the manufacturer. Add mashed garlic at the Raisin/Nut signal.

Select Basic/White cycle. Use Medium or Light crust color. Do not use delay cycles. Remove baked bread from pan, and cool on wire rack.

Roasted Garlic

Heat oven to 350°. Carefully peel away paperlike skin from around garlic bulbs, leaving just enough to hold bulb intact. Trim tops of garlic bulbs about 1/2 inch to expose cloves. Place bulbs, stem ends down, on 12-inch square of aluminum foil. Drizzle each bulb with 2 teaspoons olive or vegetable oil. Wrap securely in foil; place in pie plate or shallow baking pan. Bake 45 to 50 minutes or until garlic is tender when pierced with toothpick or fork. Cool slightly. Gently squeeze garlic out of cloves.

■ 1 Slice: 150 calories (20 calories from fat); 2g fat (0g saturated); 0mg cholesterol; 180mg sodium; 30g carbohydrate (1g dietary fiber); 4g protein

Roasted Garlic Bread

Gingery Bread

1 1/2-Pound Recipe (12 slices)		2-Pound Recipe (16 slices)
3/4 cup	Water	1 1/3 cups
1/4 cup	Molasses	1/4 cup
2 tablespoons	Margarine or butter, softened	2 tablespoons
1 teaspoon	Grated lemon peel	1 teaspoon
3 cups	Bread flour	4 cups
1 teaspoon	Salt	1 1/2 teaspoons
1 teaspoon	Ground ginger	1 teaspoon
1/2 teaspoon	Ground cinnamon	1/2 teaspoon
1 1/2 teaspoons	Bread machine or quick active dry yeast	1 teaspoon

Make 1 1/2-Pound Recipe with bread machines that use 3 cups flour, or make 2-Pound Recipe with bread machines that use 4 cups flour.

Measure carefully, placing all ingredients in bread machine pan in the order recommended by the manufacturer.

Select Basic/White cycle. Use Medium or Light crust color. Remove baked bread from pan, and cool on wire rack.

■ 1 Slice: 155 calories (20 calories from fat); 2g fat (0g saturated); 0mg cholesterol; 200mg sodium; 31g carbohydrate (1g dietary fiber); 4g protein

SUCCESS TIP

We found from our testing that for good texture and volume, slightly less yeast is needed in the 2-pound loaf than is needed in the 1 1/2-pound loaf.

DID YOU KNOW?

Mild molasses, also known as light molasses, comes from the first boiling of syrup from sugar cane or sugar beets. It is lighter in color and flavor. Full molasses, also known as dark molasses, comes from the second boiling and is darker, thicker and less sweet. Either molasses will work in this bread, but the mild molasses will give you a spicier flavor that will not overshadow the ginger and cinnamon.

SANDWICH BOARD

An Open-Face Pear Sandwich is a tasty treat to eat with a comforting cup of steaming tea. Spread a slice of Gingery Bread with softened cream cheese, and layer with thin slices of fresh pear. If you are a true ginger lover, try sprinkling some finely chopped crystallized ginger over the top. This sandwich also is good with sliced apples.

Gingery Bread

Raisin Cinnamon Bread

SUCCESS TIP

We found from our testing that for good texture and volume, slightly less yeast is needed in the 2-pound loaf than is needed in the 1 1/2-pound loaf.

SUCCESS TIP

Be sure to measure the cinnamon accurately for this recipe. A "pinch" of some spices, such as cinnamon, ginger and cardamom, actually helps the yeast to grow. But it is important to measure carefully, since too much of a good thing, like cinnamon, causes the yeast to slow down rather than grow.

SUCCESS TIP

If your bread machine doesn't have a Raisin/Nut signal, add the raisins 5 to 10 minutes before the last kneading cycle ends. Check your bread machine's use-and-care book to find out how long the last cycle runs.

1 1/2-Pound Recipe *(12 slices)*		*2-Pound Recipe* *(16 slices)*
1 cup plus 2 tablespoons	Water	1 1/2 cups
2 tablespoons	Margarine or butter, softened	2 tablespoons
3 cups	Bread flour	4 cups
3 tablespoons	Sugar	1/4 cup
1 1/2 teaspoons	Salt	1 1/2 teaspoons
1 teaspoon	Ground cinnamon	1 1/2 teaspoons
2 1/2 teaspoons	Bread machine or quick active dry yeast	1 1/4 teaspoons
3/4 cup	Raisins	1 cup

Make 1 1/2-Pound Recipe with bread machines that use 3 cups flour, or make 2-Pound Recipe with bread machines that use 4 cups flour.

Measure carefully, placing all ingredients except raisins in bread machine pan in the order recommended by the manufacturer. Add raisins at the Raisin/Nut signal.

Select Sweet or Basic/White cycle. Use Medium or Light crust color. Remove baked bread from pan, and cool on wire rack.

■ 1 Slice: 175 calories (20 calories from fat); 2g fat (0g saturated); 0mg cholesterol; 290mg sodium; 37g carbohydrate (2g dietary fiber); 4g protein

Raisin Cinnamon Bread

Honey Mustard Bread

TRY THIS

Have you noticed the variety of mustards that are now available in your grocery store? You can use any variety of mustard in this recipe! Try a honey mustard for an added touch of sweetness, a spicy brown or Dijon for a spicier flavor.

DID YOU KNOW?

A honey's color and flavor is derived from the nectar of the flower. There are many different honeys; two popular flavors are clover and orange blossom. Look for honeys that are indigenous to your region.

1 1/2-Pound Recipe *(12 slices)*		*2-Pound Recipe* *(16 slices)*
3/4 cup plus 1 tablespoon	Water	1 cup
2 tablespoons	Honey	3 tablespoons
2 tablespoons	Mustard	3 tablespoons
2 tablespoons	Margarine or butter, softened	3 tablespoons
3 cups	Bread flour	4 cups
1/2 teaspoon	Salt	3/4 teaspoon
1/2 teaspoon	Paprika	1 teaspoon
1 1/2 teaspoons	Bread machine or quick active dry yeast	1 3/4 teaspoons

Make 1 1/2-Pound Recipe with bread machines that use 3 cups flour, or make 2-Pound Recipe with bread machines that use 4 cups flour.

Measure carefully, placing all ingredients in bread machine pan in the order recommended by the manufacturer.

Select Basic/White cycle. Use Medium or Light crust color. Do not use delay cycles. Remove baked bread from pan, and cool on wire rack.

■ 1 Slice: 145 calories (20 calories from fat); 2g fat (1g saturated); 0mg cholesterol; 150mg sodium; 29g carbohydrate (1g dietary fiber); 4g protein

Cheesy Mustard Pretzel Bread

1 1/2-Pound Recipe (12 slices)		2-Pound Recipe (16 slices)
1 cup	Water	1 cup plus 2 tablespoons
1 tablespoon	Vegetable oil	1 1/2 tablespoons
2 tablespoons	Mustard	3 tablespoons
3 cups	Bread flour	4 cups
1 tablespoon	Sugar	2 tablespoons
1 teaspoon	Salt	1 teaspoon
2 teaspoons	Bread machine or quick active dry yeast	2 teaspoons
1/2 cup	Shredded sharp Cheddar cheese	2/3 cup
	Coarse salt, if desired	

Make 1 1/2-Pound Recipe with bread machines that use 3 cups flour, or make 2-Pound Recipe with bread machines that use 4 cups flour.

Measure carefully, placing all ingredients except cheese and coarse salt in bread machine pan in the order recommended by the manufacturer. Add cheese at the Raisin/Nut signal.

Select Basic/White cycle. Use Medium or Light crust color. Do not use delay cycles. Before baking cycle begins, carefully brush top of dough with water and sprinkle with coarse salt. Remove baked bread from pan, and cool on wire rack.

■ 1 Slice: 155 calories (30 calories from fat); 3g fat (1g saturated); 5mg cholesterol; 260mg sodium; 28g carbohydrate (1g dietary fiber); 5g protein

SUCCESS TIP

We found from our testing that the same amount of yeast is needed for both the 1 1/2-pound and 2-pound loaves.

SUCCESS TIP

If your bread machine doesn't have a Raisin/Nut signal, add the cheese 5 to 10 minutes before the last kneading cycle ends. Check your bread machine's use-and-care book to find out how long the last cycle runs.

Parmesan Sun-Dried Tomato Bread

1 1/2-Pound Recipe (12 slices)		2-Pound Recipe (16 slices)
1 cup plus 2 tablespoons	Water	1 1/4 cups
3 cups	Bread flour	4 cups
1/2 cup	Shredded Parmesan cheese	3/4 cup
1 1/2 cloves	Crushed garlic	2 cloves
2 tablespoons	Sugar	3 tablespoons
1 teaspoon	Salt	1 1/4 teaspoons
1 1/2 teaspoons	Dried oregano leaves	2 1/4 teaspoons
2 teaspoons	Bread machine or quick active dry yeast	2 1/4 teaspoons
1/3 cup	Sun-dried tomatoes (packed in oil), drained and coarsely chopped	2/3 cup

Make 1 1/2-Pound Recipe with bread machines that use 3 cups flour, or make 2-Pound Recipe with bread machines that use 4 cups flour.

Measure carefully, placing all ingredients except tomatoes in bread machine pan in the order recommended by the manufacturer. Add tomatoes at the Raisin/Nut signal.

Select Basic/White cycle. Use Medium or Light crust color. Do not use delay cycles. Remove baked bread from pan, and cool on wire rack.

■ 1 Slice: 150 calories (20 calories from fat); 2g fat (1g saturated); 5mg cholesterol; 270mg sodium; 29g carbohydrate (1g dietary fiber); 5g protein

Parmesan Sun-Dried Tomato Bread

Beer Bacon Bread

SUCCESS TIP

We found from our testing that for good texture and volume, slightly less yeast is needed in the 2-pound loaf than is needed in the 1 1/2-pound loaf.

SUCCESS TIP

For flat beer, open the can or bottle and let it stand about 1 hour before using. The flat beer is necessary for a good-textured bread.

SUCCESS TIP

If your bread machine doesn't have a Raisin/Nut signal, add the bacon 5 to 10 minutes before the last kneading cycle ends. Check your bread machine's use-and-care book to find out how long the last cycle runs.

1 1/2-Pound Recipe (12 slices)		*2-Pound Recipe (16 slices)*
3/4 cup	Flat beer or nonalcoholic beer	3/4 cup
1/2 cup	Water	2/3 cup
1/4 cup	Chopped green onions	1/4 cup
2 tablespoons	Mustard	2 tablespoons
1 tablespoon	Margarine or butter, softened	1 tablespoon
3 1/4 cups	Bread flour	4 1/4 cups
1 tablespoon	Sugar	1 tablespoon
3/4 teaspoon	Salt	1 teaspoon
1 3/4 teaspoons	Bread machine or quick active dry yeast	1 1/2 teaspoons
1/3 cup	Crumbled cooked bacon	1/2 cup

Make 1 1/2-Pound Recipe with bread machines that use at least 3 cups flour, or make 2-Pound Recipe with bread machines that use at least 4 cups flour.

Measure carefully, placing all ingredients except bacon in bread machine pan in the order recommended by the manufacturer. Add bacon at the Raisin/Nut signal.

Select Basic/White cycle. Use Medium or Light crust color. Do not use delay cycles. Remove baked bread from pan, and cool on wire rack.

■ 1 Slice: 165 calories (25 calories from fat); 3g fat (1g saturated); 2mg cholesterol; 210mg sodium; 30g carbohydrate (1g dietary fiber); 5g protein

Beer Bacon Bread

Caraway Cheese Bread

1 1/2-Pound Recipe (12 slices)		2-Pound Recipe (16 slices)
1 cup	Water	1 1/4 cups
3 cups	Bread flour	4 cups
3/4 cup	Shredded sharp Cheddar cheese	1 cup
1 1/2 teaspoons	Caraway seed	2 teaspoons
1 tablespoon	Sugar	2 tablespoons
3/4 teaspoon	Salt	1 teaspoon
1 1/2 teaspoons	Bread machine or quick active dry yeast	1 1/2 teaspoons

Make 1 1/2–Pound Recipe with bread machines that use 3 cups flour, or make 2–Pound Recipe with bread machines that use 4 cups flour.

Measure carefully, placing all ingredients in bread machine pan in the order recommended by the manufacturer.

Select Basic/White cycle. Use Medium or Light crust color. Do not use delay cycles. Remove baked bread from pan, and cool on wire rack.

■ 1 Slice: 150 calories (25 calories from fat); 3g fat (2g saturated); 5mg cholesterol; 190mg sodium; 27g carbohydrate (1g dietary fiber); 5g protein

Toffee Chip Bread

1 1/2-Pound Recipe (12 slices)		2-Pound Recipe (16 slices)
2/3 cup	Water	1 1/4 cups
2 tablespoons	Margarine or butter, softened	1 tablespoon
3 cups	Bread flour	4 cups
2/3 cup	Chocolate-covered toffee chips	2/3 cup
3 tablespoons	Sugar	3 tablespoons
1 1/4 teaspoons	Salt	1 1/2 teaspoons
2 teaspoons	Bread machine or quick active dry yeast	1 3/4 teaspoons

Make 1 1/2–Pound Recipe with bread machines that use 3 cups flour, or make 2-Pound Recipe with bread machines that use 4 cups flour.

Measure carefully, placing all ingredients in bread machine pan in the order recommended by the manufacturer.

Select Sweet or Basic/White cycle. Use Medium or Light crust color. Remove baked bread from pan, and cool on wire rack.

■ 1 Slice: 205 calories (55 calories from fat); 6g fat (3g saturated); 5mg cholesterol; 300mg sodium; 35g carbohydrate (1g dietary fiber); 4g protein

SUCCESS TIP

We found from our testing that for good texture and volume, slightly less yeast is needed in the 2-pound loaf than is needed in the 1 1/2-pound loaf.

DID YOU KNOW?

You can find chocolate-covered toffee chips in the baking aisle of your supermarket. The flavor of these little pieces of toffee covered with chocolate adds a bit of sweetness to this bread.

Honey Lemon Bread

SUCCESS TIP

We found from our testing that the same amount of yeast is needed for both the 1 1/2-pound and 2-pound loaves.

TRY THIS

For a flavor change, use grated orange peel instead of the lemon peel to make Orange Honey Bread. The zip of the orange in the bread makes it great for French toast, topped with sliced bananas or blueberries, a drizzle of warm honey and a sprinkle of cinnamon.

1 1/2-Pound Recipe (12 slices)		2-Pound Recipe (16 slices)
3/4 cup plus 2 tablespoons	Water	1 cup plus 1 tablespoon
3 tablespoons	Honey	1/4 cup
2 tablespoons	Margarine or butter, softened	2 tablespoons
3 cups	Bread flour	4 cups
2 tablespoons	Dry milk	2 tablespoons
1 1/2 teaspoons	Grated lemon peel	2 teaspoons
1 teaspoon	Salt	1 1/2 teaspoons
2 teaspoons	Bread machine or quick active dry yeast	2 teaspoons

Make 1 1/2-Pound Recipe with bread machines that use 3 cups flour, or make 2-Pound Recipe with bread machines that use 4 cups flour.

Measure carefully, placing all ingredients in bread machine pan in the order recommended by the manufacturer.

Select Sweet or Basic/White cycle. Use Medium or Light crust color. Do not use delay cycles. Remove baked bread from pan, and cool on wire rack.

◼ 1 Slice: 145 calories (20 calories from fat); 2g fat (0g saturated); 0mg cholesterol; 220mg sodium; 29g carbohydrate (1g dietary fiber); 4g protein

Brandied Pumpkin Bread (page 104) and Honey Lemon Bread

Orange Cappuccino Bread

SUCCESS TIP

We found from our testing that the same amount of yeast is needed for both the 1 1/2-pound and 2-pound loaves.

TRY THIS

Coffee lovers may want to use granules of instant espresso instead of regular coffee.

SANDWICH BOARD

Now you can get your morning coffee two ways—one in your cup and the other in your morning toast! Top a warm piece of coffee-flavored toast with orange marmalade or spread generously with butter or cream cheese. It's a delicious way to welcome the day.

1 1/2-Pound Recipe (12 slices)		2-Pound Recipe (16 slices)
1 cup	Water	1 cup plus 3 tablespoons
1 tablespoon	Instant coffee granules	2 tablespoons
2 tablespoons	Margarine or butter, softened	2 tablespoons
1 teaspoon	Grated orange peel	1 1/4 teaspoons
3 cups	Bread flour	4 cups
2 tablespoons	Dry milk	2 tablespoons
1/4 cup	Sugar	1/3 cup
1 1/4 teaspoons	Salt	1 1/2 teaspoons
2 1/4 teaspoons	Bread machine or quick active dry yeast	2 1/4 teaspoons

Make 1 1/2-Pound Recipe with bread machines that use 3 cups flour, or make 2-Pound Recipe with bread machines that use 4 cups flour.

Measure carefully, placing all ingredients in bread machine pan in the order recommended by the manufacturer.

Select Sweet or Basic/White cycle. Use Light crust color. Remove baked bread from pan, and cool on wire rack.

■ 1 Slice: 155 calories (20 calories from fat); 2g fat (0g saturated); 0mg cholesterol; 270mg sodium; 31g carbohydrate (1g dietary fiber); 4g protein

Orange Cappuccino Bread

Chocolate Walnut Bread

SUCCESS TIP

We found from our testing that the same amount of yeast is needed for both the 1 1/2-pound and 2-pound loaves.

SUCCESS TIP

Because you will add the chocolate chips with all the other ingredients, they will break up during kneading and will melt during baking, so you will have a chocolate bread, not a chocolate chip bread.

TRY THIS

Mint-chocolate chips or milk chocolate chips will give you a different flavor of chocolate bread. Not in the mood for chocolate? Try the same amount of butterscotch-flavored chips.

1 1/2-Pound Recipe (12 slices)		2-Pound Recipe (16 slices)
1 egg plus enough water to equal 3/4 cup plus 2 tablespoons	Egg	1 egg plus enough water to equal 1 1/4 cups
1/2 teaspoon	Salt	1 teaspoon
3 tablespoons	Sugar	1/4 cup
1 tablespoon	Margarine or butter, softened	2 tablespoons
1/2 teaspoon	Vanilla	1 teaspoon
2 1/4 cups	Bread flour	3 1/4 cups
1 tablespoon	Dry milk	1 tablespoon plus 1 1/2 teaspoons
3/4 cup	Semisweet chocolate chips	1 cup
1/4 cup	Walnut halves	1/2 cup
1 teaspoon	Bread machine or quick active dry yeast	1 teaspoon

Make 1 1/2-Pound Recipe with bread machines that use 3 cups flour, or make 2-Pound Recipe with bread machines that use 4 cups flour.

Measure carefully, placing all ingredients in bread machine pan in the order recommended by the manufacturer.

Select Sweet or Basic/White cycle. Use Medium or Light crust color. Do not use delay cycles. Remove baked bread from pan, and cool on wire rack.

■ 1 Slice: 180 calories (55 calories from fat); 6g fat (2g saturated); 20mg cholesterol; 110mg sodium; 30g carbohydrate (2g dietary fiber); 4g protein

Chocolate Mint Bread

1 1/2-Pound Recipe (12 slices)		2-Pound Recipe (16 slices)
1 cup plus 2 tablespoons	Water	1 1/4 cups plus 2 tablespoons
2 tablespoons	Margarine or butter, softened	2 tablespoons
3 cups	Bread flour	4 cups
2/3 cup	Mint-chocolate chips	2/3 cup
1/4 cup	Sugar	1/3 cup
1 teaspoon	Salt	1 1/4 teaspoons
2 teaspoons	Bread machine or quick active dry yeast	2 1/2 teaspoons

Make 1 1/2-Pound Recipe with bread machines that use 3 cups flour, or make 2-Pound Recipe with bread machines that use 4 cups flour.

Measure carefully, placing all ingredients in bread machine pan in the order recommended by the manufacturer.

Select Sweet or Basic/White cycle. Use Medium or Light crust color. Remove baked bread from pan, and cool on wire rack.

■ 1 Slice: 200 calories (45 calories from fat); 5g fat (2g saturated); 2mg cholesterol; 220mg sodium; 36g carbohydrate (1g dietary fiber); 4g protein

TRY THIS

If you don't have mint-chocolate chips, you can use semisweet chocolate chips and mint extract. Use 2/3 cup chips for either loaf, and use 1/8 teaspoon extract for the 1 1/2-pound loaf and 1/4 teaspoon for the 2-pound loaf. Or use just the semisweet chocolate chips for a chocolate bread.

SANDWICH BOARD

Make a Grilled Banana Peanut Butter on homemade bread made with semisweet chocolate chips. Spread 2 slices of bread with peanut butter—creamy or crunchy. Place slices of banana on one slice of bread, and top with the remaining slice. Butter the outside of the sandwich, then cook over medium heat until it's toasted and the peanut butter is melted, which will take about 8 minutes. Milk washes this sandwich down perfectly.

Vanilla Sour Cream Bread

1 1/2-Pound Recipe (12 slices)		2-Pound Recipe (16 slices)
1/2 cup	Water	2/3 cup
1 tablespoon	Vanilla	1 1/2 tablespoons
1/3 cup	Sour cream	1/3 cup
1	Egg	1
1 tablespoon	Margarine or butter, softened	1 tablespoon
3 cups	Bread flour	4 cups
3 tablespoons	Sugar	1/4 cup
1 1/4 teaspoons	Salt	1 1/2 teaspoons
2 teaspoons	Bread machine or quick active dry yeast	2 teaspoons

Make 1 1/2-Pound Recipe with bread machines that use 3 cups flour, or make 2-Pound Recipe with bread machines that use 4 cups flour.

Measure carefully, placing all ingredients in bread machine pan in the order recommended by the manufacturer.

Select Sweet or Basic/White cycle. Use Light crust color. Do not use delay cycles. Remove baked bread from pan, and cool on wire rack.

■ 1 Slice: 160 calories (25 calories from fat); 3g fat (1g saturated); 20mg cholesterol; 260mg sodium; 30g carbohydrate (1g dietary fiber); 4g protein

SUCCESS TIP

We don't recommend this recipe for bread machines that have a pan capacity of 9 to 12 cups because our results after several tests were unsatisfactory.

SUCCESS TIP

We found from our testing that the same amount of yeast is needed for both the 1 1/2-pound and 2-pound loaves.

SANDWICH BOARD

Looking for a fruity, creamy complement to this bread? Try a Cherry Nut Cheese Sandwich, or create your own combination of cream cheese and jam. Mix a 3-ounce package of softened cream cheese with 1 tablespoon of finely chopped walnuts and 1 tablespoon of honey. Spread it on a slice of bread, and top with cherry preserves or jam.

Vanilla Sour Cream Bread

Wholesome Grain Loaves

Cranberry Corn Bread (page 88)

Honey Whole Wheat Bread

1 1/2-Pound Recipe (12 slices)		2-Pound Recipe (16 slices)
1 cup plus 1 tablespoon	Water	1 1/2 cups
1 1/2 teaspoons	Salt	2 teaspoons
1/4 cup	Honey	1/3 cup
1 1/2 cups	Bread flour	2 1/4 cups
1 1/2 cups	Whole wheat flour	2 cups
1 tablespoon plus 1 1/2 teaspoons	Shortening	2 tablespoons
1 tablespoon	Dry milk	2 tablespoons
1 teaspoon	Bread machine or quick active dry yeast	1 teaspoon

Make 1 1/2-Pound Recipe with bread machines that use 3 cups flour, or make 2-Pound Recipe with bread machines that use at least 4 cups flour.

Measure carefully, placing all ingredients in bread machine pan in the order recommended by the manufacturer.

Select Whole Wheat or Basic/White cycle. Use Medium or Light crust color. Do not use delay cycles. Remove baked bread from pan, and cool on wire rack.

■ 1 Slice: 145 calories (20 calories from fat); 2g fat (0g saturated); 0mg cholesterol; 270mg sodium; 30g carbohydrate (2g dietary fiber); 4g protein

Toasted Almond Whole Wheat Bread

1 1/2-Pound Recipe (12 slices)		2-Pound Recipe (16 slices)
1 cup plus 2 tablespoons	Water	1 1/4 cups
3 tablespoons	Honey	1/4 cup
2 tablespoons	Margarine or butter, softened	2 tablespoons
1 1/2 cups	Bread flour	2 cups
1 1/2 cups	Whole wheat flour	2 cups
1/4 cup	Slivered almonds, toasted (see Success Tip)	1/4 cup
1 teaspoon	Salt	1 1/2 teaspoons
1 1/2 teaspoons	Bread machine or quick active dry yeast	1 1/2 teaspoons

Make 1 1/2-Pound Recipe with bread machines that use 3 cups flour, or make 2-Pound Recipe with bread machines that use 4 cups flour.

Measure carefully, placing all ingredients in bread machine pan in the order recommended by the manufacturer.

Select Whole Wheat or Basic/White cycle. Use Medium or Light crust color. Do not use delay cycles. Remove baked bread from pan, and cool on wire rack.

■ 1 Slice: 160 calories (35 calories from fat); 4g fat (1g saturated); 0mg cholesterol; 200mg sodium; 29g carbohydrate (2g dietary fiber); 4g protein

SUCCESS TIP

We found from our testing that the same amount of yeast is needed for both the 1 1/2-pound and 2-pound loaves.

SUCCESS TIP

Toast the almonds by sprinkling them in a heavy skillet. Cook over medium-low heat, stirring frequently, until golden brown, about 5 to 7 minutes. Pour them out of the skillet so they don't continue to brown, and let them cool before using.

Cinnamon Honey Wheat Bread

Cinnamon has a property that tends to absorb moisture in bread, so measure the ground cinnamon carefully rather than guessing the amount. Also, check the dough after about 5 minutes of kneading. If the dough looks too dry and a soft ball isn't forming, add water, 1 teaspoon at a time.

Leftover cinnamon-flavored bread makes wonderful bread pudding. You can leave the cinnamon out of the pudding recipe because it is already baked in the bread. For a flavor twist, use dried cranberries or cherries for the raisins. Or add nuts instead of the raisins, and serve with warm maple syrup.

1 1/2-Pound Recipe (12 slices)		2-Pound Recipe (16 slices)
1 cup	Water	1 1/4 cups
3 tablespoons	Honey	1/4 cup
2 tablespoons	Margarine or butter, softened	2 tablespoons
1 1/2 cups	Bread flour	2 cups
1 1/2 cups	Whole wheat flour	2 cups
2 tablespoons	Dry milk	3 tablespoons
1 teaspoon	Ground cinnamon	1 1/4 teaspoons
1 1/2 teaspoons	Salt	1 3/4 teaspoons
2 teaspoons	Bread machine or quick active dry yeast	2 1/4 teaspoons

Make 1 1/2-Pound Recipe with bread machines that use 3 cups flour, or make 2-Pound Recipe with bread machines that use 4 cups flour.

Measure carefully, placing all ingredients in bread machine pan in the order recommended by the manufacturer.

Select Whole Wheat or Basic/White cycle. Use Medium or Light crust color. Do not use delay cycles. Remove baked bread from pan, and cool on wire rack.

■ 1 Slice: 140 calories (20 calories from fat); 2g fat (0g saturated); 0mg cholesterol; 320mg sodium; 29g carbohydrate (2g dietary fiber); 4g protein

Citrus Whole Wheat Bread

1 1/2-Pound Recipe (12 slices)		2-Pound Recipe (16 slices)
3/4 cup	Water	3/4 cup plus 2 tablespoons
1/2 cup	Orange juice	2/3 cup
2 tablespoons	Margarine or butter, softened	2 tablespoons
1 2/3 cups	Bread flour	2 cups
1 2/3 cups	Whole wheat flour	2 cups
3 tablespoons	Wheat germ	1/4 cup
2 tablespoons	Dry milk	2 tablespoons
3 tablespoons	Sugar	1/4 cup
1 1/2 teaspoons	Salt	1 3/4 teaspoons
1 1/4 teaspoons	Grated lemon peel	1 1/2 teaspoons
3/4 teaspoon	Grated lime peel	1 teaspoon
2 teaspoons	Bread machine or quick active dry yeast	2 teaspoons

Make 1 1/2-Pound Recipe with bread machines that use at least 3 cups flour, or make 2-Pound Recipe with bread machines that use 4 cups flour.

Measure carefully, placing all ingredients in bread machine pan in the order recommended by the manufacturer.

Select Whole Wheat or Basic/White cycle. Use Medium or Light crust color. Do not use delay cycles. Remove baked bread from pan, and cool on wire rack.

■ 1 Slice: 165 calories (25 calories from fat); 3g fat (1g saturated); 0mg cholesterol; 320mg sodium; 32g carbohydrate (3g dietary fiber); 5g protein

SUCCESS TIP

We found from our testing that the same amount of yeast is needed for both the 1 1/2-pound and 2-pound loaves.

SUCCESS TIP

Fresh lemon or lime peel should be grated from only the outermost colored skin layer of the fruit. The white layer under the skin, called the pith, is bitter; be careful not to grate too deeply to avoid having the pith become part of your grated peel.

SUCCESS TIP

To get the most juice out of an orange, roll a room-temperature orange on a countertop before squeezing. This helps break down its tissue, so more juice can be released.

Golden Raisin Bread

SUCCESS TIP

We found from our testing that for good texture and volume, slightly less yeast is needed in the 2-pound loaf than is needed in the 1 1/2-pound loaf.

SUCCESS TIP

If your bread machine doesn't have a Raisin/Nut signal, add the raisins 5 to 10 minutes before the last kneading cycle ends. Check your bread machine's use-and-care book to find out how long the last cycle runs.

TRY THIS

Dried cranberries used instead of the golden raisins would add a slight tart flavor to this bread. Or use regular dark raisins instead of the golden ones for the same sweet flavor and a nice color contrast.

1 1/2-Pound Recipe (12 slices)		2-Pound Recipe (16 slices)
1 cup plus 2 tablespoons	Water	1 1/4 cups
1/4 cup	Honey	1/4 cup
2 tablespoons	Margarine or butter, softened	2 tablespoons
2 cups	Bread flour	2 1/2 cups
1 1/4 cups	Whole wheat flour	1 1/2 cups
1 1/2 teaspoons	Salt	1 1/2 teaspoons
3/4 teaspoon	Ground nutmeg	1 teaspoon
1 1/2 teaspoons	Bread machine or quick active dry yeast	2 teaspoons
1/2 cup	Golden raisins	2/3 cup

Make 1 1/2-Pound Recipe with bread machines that use at least 3 cups flour, or make 2-Pound Recipe with bread machines that use 4 cups flour.

Measure carefully, placing all ingredients except raisins in bread machine pan in the order recommended by the manufacturer. Add raisins at the Raisin/Nut signal.

Select Whole Wheat or Basic/White cycle. Use Medium or Light crust color. Do not use delay cycles. Remove baked bread from pan, and cool on wire rack.

■ 1 Slice: 180 calories (20 calories from fat); 2g fat (0g saturated); 0mg cholesterol; 290mg sodium; 38g carbohydrate (2g dietary fiber); 4g protein

Golden Raisin Bread

Herb and Crunch Wheat Bread

SUCCESS TIP

We found from our testing that the same amount of yeast is needed for both the 1 1/2-pound and 2-pound loaves.

SUCCESS TIP

If your bread machine doesn't have a Raisin/Nut signal, add the nuts 5 to 10 minutes before the last kneading cycle ends. Check your bread machine's use-and-care book to find out how long the last cycle runs.

DID YOU KNOW?

The sunflower is the state flower of Kansas, but California, Minnesota and North Dakota are the largest producers in the States. Sunflower nuts are available raw, can be oil-roasted or dry-roasted. Dry-roasted nuts are lower in fat because they contain only the natural oil in the nuts and no oil from roasting.

1 1/2-Pound Recipe (12 slices)		2-Pound Recipe (16 slices)
1 1/4 cups	Water	1 1/2 cups
1 1/2 cups	Bread flour	2 cups
1 1/2 cups	Whole wheat flour	2 cups
2 tablespoons	Sugar	2 tablespoons
2 tablespoons	Dry milk	2 tablespoons
2 tablespoons	Margarine or butter, softened	2 tablespoons
1 1/2 teaspoons	Salt	2 teaspoons
1 1/2 teaspoons	Dried basil leaves	2 teaspoons
1 teaspoon	Dried thyme leaves	1 teaspoon
2 teaspoons	Bread machine or quick active dry yeast	2 teaspoons
1/2 cup	Dry-roasted sunflower nuts	2/3 cup

Make 1 1/2-Pound Recipe with bread machines that use 3 cups flour, or make 2-Pound Recipe with bread machines that use 4 cups flour.

Measure carefully, placing all ingredients except nuts in bread machine pan in the order recommended by the manufacturer. Add nuts at the Raisin/Nut signal.

Select Basic/White cycle. Use Medium or Light crust color. Remove baked bread from pan, and cool on wire rack.

■ 1 Slice: 170 calories (45 calories from fat); 5g fat (1g saturated); 0mg cholesterol; 340mg sodium; 28g carbohydrate (2g dietary fiber); 5g protein

Herb and Crunch Wheat Bread

Dill Wheat Bread

SUCCESS TIP

We found from our testing that the same amount of yeast is needed for both the 1 1/2-pound and 2-pound loaves.

TRY THIS

Your guests will love it if you make a "dip bowl" out of a loaf of this bread. Cut off the top one-third of the loaf and put it aside. Hollow out the loaf to form a bowl. Cut the removed chunks of bread and reserved top into cubes. Fill the bowl with your favorite spinach dip or other tasty dip, and serve with the bread cubes.

1 1/2-Pound Recipe (12 slices)		2-Pound Recipe (16 slices)
1 cup	Water	1 1/4 cups
2 tablespoons	Honey	2 tablespoons
2 tablespoons	Margarine or butter, softened	2 tablespoons
2 cups	Bread flour	2 1/4 cups
1 1/2 cups	Whole wheat flour	1 2/3 cups
2 tablespoons	Dry milk	2 tablespoons
1 teaspoon	Salt	1 1/4 teaspoons
1 teaspoon	Dried dill weed	1 1/2 teaspoons
1 teaspoon	Caraway seed	1 1/2 teaspoons
2 teaspoons	Bread machine or quick active dry yeast	2 teaspoons

Make 1 1/2-Pound Recipe with bread machines that use at least 3 cups flour, or make 2-Pound Recipe with bread machines that use 4 cups flour.

Measure carefully, placing all ingredients in bread machine pan in the order recommended by the manufacturer.

Select Whole Wheat or Basic/White cycle. Use Medium or Light crust color. Do not use delay cycles. Remove baked bread from pan, and cool on wire rack.

■ 1 Slice: 165 calories (25 calories from fat); 3g fat (1g saturated); 0mg cholesterol; 220mg sodium; 32g carbohydrate (2g dietary fiber); 5g protein

Dill Wheat Bread

Golden Raisin and Rosemary Wheat Bread

1 1/2-Pound Recipe (12 slices)		2-Pound Recipe (16 slices)
1 1/4 cups	Water	1 1/3 cups plus 1 tablespoon
2 tablespoons	Margarine or butter, softened	2 tablespoons
1 1/2 cups	Bread flour	2 cups
1 1/2 cups	Whole wheat flour	2 cups
2 tablespoons	Dry milk	2 tablespoons
3/4 teaspoon	Crumbled dried rosemary leaves	1 teaspoon
2 tablespoons	Sugar	2 tablespoons
1 1/2 teaspoons	Salt	1 3/4 teaspoons
1 3/4 teaspoons	Bread machine or quick active dry yeast	2 1/4 teaspoons
3/4 cup	Golden raisins	3/4 cup

Make 1 1/2-Pound Recipe with bread machines that use 3 cups flour, or make 2-Pound Recipe with bread machines that use 4 cups flour.

Measure carefully, placing all ingredients except raisins in bread machine pan in the order recommended by the manufacturer. Add raisins at the Raisin/Nut signal.

Select Whole Wheat or Basic/White cycle. Use Medium or Light crust color. Remove baked bread from pan, and cool on wire rack.

▪ 1 Slice: 160 calories (20 calories from fat); 2g fat (0g saturated); 0mg cholesterol; 320mg sodium; 34g carbohydrate (3g dietary fiber); 4g protein

Seeded Whole Wheat Bread

1 1/2-Pound Recipe (12 slices)		2-Pound Recipe (16 slices)
1 cup plus 1 tablespoon	Water	1 1/4 cups plus 2 tablespoons
2 tablespoons	Margarine or butter, softened	2 tablespoons
1 1/2 cups	Bread flour	2 cups
1 1/2 cups	Whole wheat flour	2 cups
2 tablespoons	Dry milk	3 tablespoons
2 tablespoons	Sugar	3 tablespoons
1 teaspoon	Dill seed	1 1/2 teaspoons
1 1/2 teaspoons	Sesame seed	2 teaspoons
1 teaspoon	Caraway seed	1 1/2 teaspoons
1 1/2 teaspoons	Salt	1 3/4 teaspoons
2 teaspoons	Bread machine or quick active dry yeast	2 teaspoons

Make 1 1/2-Pound Recipe with bread machines that use 3 cups flour, or make 2-Pound Recipe with bread machines that use 4 cups flour.

Measure carefully, placing all ingredients in bread machine pan in the order recommended by the manufacturer.

Select Whole Wheat or Basic/White cycle. Use Medium or Light crust color. Remove baked bread from pan, and cool on wire rack.

■ 1 Slice: 145 calories (25 calories from fat); 3g fat (1g saturated); 0mg cholesterol; 320mg sodium; 27g carbohydrate (2g dietary fiber); 4g protein

SUCCESS TIP

We found from our testing that the same amount of yeast is needed for both the 1 1/2-pound and 2-pound loaves.

TRY THIS

We selected dill, sesame and caraway seed for this recipe, but other combinations of seed would work also. Consider anise seed, fennel seed, celery seed, coriander seed and mustard seed.

Nutty Prune Wheat Bread

SUCCESS TIP

We found from our testing that the same amount of yeast is needed for both the 1 1/2-pound and 2-pound loaves.

SUCCESS TIP

If your bread machine doesn't have a Raisin/Nut signal, add the prunes and walnuts 5 to 10 minutes before the last kneading cycle ends. Check your bread machine's use-and-care book to find out how long the last cycle runs.

TRY THIS

Toast slices of this prune-studded bread to serve at breakfast with fluffy scrambled eggs, Canadian-style bacon and fresh-squeezed orange juice. Serve with lemon curd or orange marmalade.

1 1/2-Pound Recipe (12 slices)		2-Pound Recipe (16 slices)
1 cup	Water	1 1/3 cups
2 tablespoons	Margarine or butter, softened	2 tablespoons
1 1/2 cups	Bread flour	2 cups
1 1/2 cups	Whole wheat flour	2 cups
3 tablespoons	Packed brown sugar	1/4 cup
2 tablespoons	Dry milk	2 tablespoons
1 teaspoon	Salt	1 1/4 teaspoons
2 teaspoons	Bread machine or quick active dry yeast	2 teaspoons
1/2 cup	Coarsely chopped pitted prunes	2/3 cup
1/3 cup	Chopped walnuts	1/2 cup

Make 1 1/2-Pound Recipe with bread machines that use 3 cups flour, or make 2-Pound Recipe with bread machines that use 4 cups flour.

Measure carefully, placing all ingredients except prunes and walnuts in bread machine pan in the order recommended by the manufacturer. Add prunes and walnuts at the Raisin/Nut signal.

Select Whole Wheat or Basic/White cycle. Use Medium crust color. Remove baked bread from pan, and cool on wire rack.

■ 1 Slice: 185 calories (45 calories from fat); 5g fat (1g saturated); 0mg cholesterol; 230mg sodium; 33g carbohydrate (3g dietary fiber); 5g protein

Nutty Prune Wheat Bread

Zucchini Wheat Bread

1 1/2-Pound Recipe *(12 slices)*		*2-Pound Recipe* *(16 slices)*
3/4 cup plus 1 tablespoon	Water	1 cup
1/2 cup	Shredded zucchini	2/3 cup
2 tablespoons	Margarine or butter, softened	2 tablespoons
1 1/2 cups	Bread flour	2 cups
1 1/2 cups	Whole wheat flour	2 cups
2 tablespoons	Dry milk	2 tablespoons
1/4 cup	Sugar	1/3 cup
1/2 teaspoon	Ground cinnamon	3/4 teaspoon
1/4 teaspoon	Ground cloves	1/2 teaspoon
1 teaspoon	Salt	1 teaspoon
2 teaspoons	Bread machine or quick active dry yeast	2 teaspoons
1/4 cup	Chopped walnuts	1/3 cup

Make 1 1/2-Pound Recipe with bread machines that use 3 cups flour, or make 2-Pound Recipe with bread machines that use 4 cups flour.

Measure carefully, placing all ingredients except walnuts in bread machine pan in the order recommended by the manufacturer. Add walnuts at the Raisin/Nut signal.

Select Whole Wheat or Basic/White cycle. Use Medium or Light crust color. Do not use delay cycles. Remove baked bread from pan, and cool on wire rack.

■ 1 Slice: 150 calories (30 calories from fat); 4g fat (1g saturated); 0mg cholesterol; 230mg sodium; 28g carbohydrate (3g dietary fiber); 5g protein

Zucchini Wheat Bread

Wild Rice and Apple Bread

SUCCESS TIP

If your bread machine doesn't have a Raisin/Nut signal, add the apple 5 to 10 minutes before the last kneading cycle ends. Check your bread machine's use-and-care book to find out how long the last cycle runs.

TRY THIS

Another rice, such as brown or basmati, can be used instead of the wild rice. Or if you have several types of leftover cooked rice, mix them together for the amount needed in the recipe. This bread is also great when making stuffing.

SANDWICH BOARD

Layer some fresh turkey, spicy mustard, lettuce and tomato in between thick slices of this bread. You can't find a better sandwich!

1 1/2-Pound Recipe (12 slices)		2-Pound Recipe (16 slices)
1 cup	Water	1 1/4 cups
1 tablespoon	Molasses	2 tablespoons
1 tablespoon	Vegetable oil	2 tablespoons
1 1/2 cups	Bread flour	2 cups
1 1/2 cups	Whole wheat flour	2 cups
1/2 cup	Cooked wild rice	2/3 cup
1 teaspoon	Dried thyme leaves	1 1/2 teaspoons
1 teaspoon	Salt	1 1/2 teaspoons
1 1/4 teaspoons	Bread machine or quick active dry yeast	1 3/4 teaspoons
2/3 cup	Chopped unpeeled cooking apple	3/4 cup

Make 1 1/2–Pound Recipe with bread machines that use 3 cups flour, or make 2–Pound Recipe with bread machines that use 4 cups flour.

Measure carefully, placing all ingredients except apple in bread machine pan in the order recommended by the manufacturer. Add apple at the Raisin/Nut signal.

Select Whole Wheat or Basic/White cycle. Use Medium or Light crust color. Do not use delay cycles. Do not use rapid cycle. Remove baked bread from pan, and cool on wire rack.

■ 1 Slice: 155 calories (20 calories from fat); 2g fat (0g saturated); 0mg cholesterol; 200mg sodium; 32g carbohydrate (3g dietary fiber); 5g protein

Wild Rice and Apple Bread

Pumpernickel Bread

Pumpernickel bread is a heavier dark bread. Our recipe uses both rye and whole wheat flours. The molasses, cocoa and coffee not only add flavor, but they increase the deep brown color of this bread.

Here's your chance to make a great Deli Corned Beef Sandwich. Spread slices of pumpernickel bread with a spicy mustard. Pile high with slices of corned beef, drained canned sauerkraut and Swiss cheese, and top with another slice of bread. Serve with big, crisp kosher dill pickles.

1 1/2-Pound Recipe (12 slices)		*2-Pound Recipe (16 slices)*
1 cup plus 2 tablespoons	Water	1 1/2 cups
1 1/2 teaspoons	Salt	2 teaspoons
1/3 cup	Molasses, full flavor	1/2 cup
2 tablespoons	Vegetable oil	2 tablespoons
1 cup plus 1 tablespoon	Rye flour	1 1/2 cups
1 cup plus 2 tablespoons	Whole wheat flour	1 1/2 cups
1 1/2 cups	Bread flour	2 cups
3 tablespoons	Baking cocoa	1/4 cup
1 1/2 teaspoons	Instant coffee granules	2 teaspoons
1 tablespoon	Caraway seed	2 tablespoons
1 teaspoon	Bread machine or quick active dry yeast	1 1/4 teaspoons

Make 1 1/2–Pound Recipe with bread machines that use at least 3 cups flour, or make 2-Pound Recipe with bread machines that use at least 4 cups flour.

Measure carefully, placing all ingredients in bread machine pan in the order recommended by the manufacturer.

Select Whole Wheat or Basic/White cycle. Use Medium or Light crust color. Remove baked bread from pan, and cool on wire rack.

■ 1 Slice: 170 calories (25 calories from fat); 3g fat (1g saturated); 0mg cholesterol; 270mg sodium; 35g carbohydrate (3g dietary fiber); 4g protein

Pumpernickel Bread

Pumpernickel Pecan Bread

1 1/2-Pound Recipe (12 slices)		2-Pound Recipe (16 slices)
1 cup plus 2 tablespoons	Water	1 1/4 cups
1/4 cup	Molasses, full flavor	1/3 cup
1 tablespoon	Margarine or butter, softened	2 tablespoons
2 cups	Bread flour	2 2/3 cups
1 1/4 cups	Rye flour	1 1/2 cups
2 tablespoons	Baking cocoa	2 tablespoons
1 1/2 teaspoons	Instant coffee granules	2 teaspoons
2 teaspoons	Salt	2 teaspoons
2 1/4 teaspoons	Bread machine or quick active dry yeast	2 3/4 teaspoons
1/3 cup	Raisins	1/2 cup
1/2 cup	Chopped pecans	2/3 cup

Make 1 1/2-Pound Recipe with bread machines that use 3 cups flour, or make 2-Pound Recipe with bread machines that use 4 cups flour.

Measure carefully, placing all ingredients except raisins and pecans in bread machine pan in the order recommended by the manufacturer. Add raisins and pecans at the Raisin/Nut signal.

Select Basic/White cycle. Use Medium or Light crust color. Remove baked bread from pan, and cool on wire rack.

■ 1 Slice: 190 calories (45 calories from fat); 5g fat (1g saturated); 0mg cholesterol; 410mg sodium; 35g carbohydrate (3g dietary fiber); 4g protein

Pumpernickel Pecan Bread

Buttermilk Rye Bread

DID YOU KNOW?

Rye flour, milled from a hardy cereal grass, is low in gluten-making protein. That is why it performs so great with bread flour, which is high in gluten-making protein. The most common type of rye flour sold in supermarkets is medium rye flour. Light and dark rye flours are available in natural foods stores or co-ops. You can use any of the three flours in this recipe.

SANDWICH BOARD

Enjoy a robust Roast Beef with Caramelized Onion Sandwich. Make the Caramelized Onions on page 106. Add enough prepared horseradish to mayonnaise to taste the way you like it. Spread some of the mayonnaise on a slice of bread. Top with thinly sliced roast beef and caramelized onions. If you like cheese, add a few slices of provolone or white Cheddar cheese. Top with another slice of bread spread with the mayonnaise.

1 1/2-Pound Recipe (12 slices)		2-Pound Recipe (16 slices)
2/3 cup	Water	1 cup
2/3 cup	Buttermilk	1 cup
2 tablespoons	Vegetable oil	2 tablespoons
1/3 cup	Mashed potato mix (dry)	1/2 cup
2 1/4 cups	Bread flour	3 cups
1 cup	Rye flour	1 1/4 cups
1 1/4 teaspoons	Salt	1 1/2 teaspoons
2 tablespoons	Packed brown sugar	2 tablespoons
1 teaspoon	Caraway seed	1 1/2 teaspoons
2 teaspoons	Bread machine or quick active dry yeast	2 1/4 teaspoons

Make 1 1/2-Pound Recipe with bread machines that use at least 3 cups flour, or make 2-Pound Recipe with bread machines that use at least 4 cups flour.

Measure carefully, placing all ingredients in bread machine pan in the order recommended by the manufacturer.

Select Basic/White cycle. Use Medium or Light crust color. Do not use delay cycles. Remove baked bread from pan, and cool on wire rack.

■ 1 Slice: 155 calories (25 calories from fat); 3g fat (1g saturated); 0mg cholesterol; 260mg sodium; 30g carbohydrate (2g dietary fiber); 4g protein

Oatmeal Bread

1 1/2-Pound Recipe (12 slices)		2-Pound Recipe (16 slices)
1 1/4 cups	Water	1 1/4 cups plus 2 tablespoons
2 tablespoons	Margarine or butter, softened	2 tablespoons
3 cups	Bread flour	4 cups
1/2 cup	Old-fashioned or quick-cooking oats	2/3 cup
3 tablespoons	Packed brown sugar	1/4 cup
2 tablespoons	Dry milk	2 tablespoons
1 1/4 teaspoons	Salt	1 1/2 teaspoons
2 teaspoons	Bread machine or quick active dry yeast	2 teaspoons

Make 1 1/2-Pound Recipe with bread machines that use 3 cups flour, or make 2-Pound Recipe with bread machines that use 4 cups flour.

Measure carefully, placing all ingredients in bread machine pan in the order recommended by the manufacturer.

Select Sweet or Basic/White cycle. Use Light crust color. Remove baked bread from pan, and cool on wire rack.

■ 1 Slice: 185 calories (25 calories from fat); 3g fat (1g saturated); 0mg cholesterol; 270mg sodium; 37g carbohydrate (2g dietary fiber); 5g protein

SUCCESS TIP

We found from our testing that the same amount of yeast is needed for both the 1 1/2-pound and 2-pound loaves.

TRY THIS

Some of us like sweet, plump raisins in our hot cooked oatmeal. If you do, you'll enjoy raisins in this oatmeal bread. Use 1/2 cup raisins for the 1 1/2-pound loaf or 2/3 cup for the 2-pound loaf. Add them at the Raisin/Nut signal or 5 to 10 minutes before the last kneading cycle ends.

Oatmeal Sunflower Bread

SUCCESS TIP

If your bread machine doesn't have a Raisin/Nut signal, add the nuts 5 to 10 minutes before the last kneading cycle ends. Check your bread machine's use-and-care book to find out how long the last cycle runs.

SANDWICH BOARD

This nutty oatmeal bread makes a fabulous Santa Fe Meatloaf Sandwich. Spread tomato jam or your favorite salsa on two slices of bread. Layer slices of cold meatloaf, Monterey Jack cheese, canned chopped green chilies, avocado slices and shredded lettuce on one slice of bread. Top with remaining slice of bread. It has a wonderfully rich, zippy flavor.

1 1/2-Pound Recipe (12 slices)		2-Pound Recipe (16 slices)
1 cup	Water	1 1/4 cups
1/4 cup	Honey	1/4 cup
2 tablespoons	Margarine or butter, softened	2 tablespoons
3 cups	Bread flour	4 cups
1/2 cup	Old-fashioned or quick-cooking oats	2/3 cup
2 tablespoons	Dry milk	2 tablespoons
1 1/4 teaspoons	Salt	1 1/4 teaspoons
2 1/4 teaspoons	Bread machine or quick active dry yeast	2 1/2 teaspoons
1/2 cup	Sunflower nuts	2/3 cup

Make 1 1/2-Pound Recipe with bread machines that use 3 cups flour, or make 2-Pound Recipe with bread machines that use 4 cups flour.

Measure carefully, placing all ingredients except nuts in bread machine pan in the order recommended by the manufacturer. Add nuts at the Raisin/Nut signal.

Select Basic/White cycle. Use Medium or Light crust color. Do not use delay cycles. Remove baked bread from pan, and cool on wire rack.

■ 1 Slice: 205 calories (45 calories from fat); 5g fat (1g saturated); 0mg cholesterol; 280mg sodium; 36g carbohydrate (2g dietary fiber); 6g protein

Oatmeal Sunflower Bread and Fiery Four-Pepper Bread (page 32)

Oat Potato Sandwich Bread

1 1/2-Pound Recipe (12 slices)		2-Pound Recipe (16 slices)
1 1/4 cups	Water	1 1/2 cups plus 1 tablespoon
1 tablespoon	Vegetable oil	1 tablespoon
2 tablespoons	Honey	3 tablespoons
3 cups	Bread flour	4 cups
1/2 cup	Mashed potato mix (dry)	2/3 cup
3/4 cup	Old-fashioned or quick-cooking oats	1 cup
1/2 teaspoon	Grated lemon peel	1 teaspoon
1/2 teaspoon	Dried thyme leaves	1 teaspoon
1 1/2 teaspoons	Salt	2 teaspoons
1 1/2 teaspoons	Bread machine or quick active dry yeast	2 teaspoons

Make 1 1/2–Pound Recipe with bread machines that use 3 cups flour, or make 2–Pound Recipe with bread machines that use 4 cups flour.

Measure carefully, placing all ingredients in bread machine pan in the order recommended by the manufacturer.

Select Basic/White cycle. Use Medium or Light crust color. Do not use delay cycles. Remove baked bread from pan, and cool on wire rack.

■ 1 Slice: 165 calories (20 calories from fat); 2g fat (0g saturated); 0mg cholesterol; 290mg sodium; 34g carbohydrate (2g dietary fiber); 5g protein

Orange Oat Cornmeal Bread

1 1/2-Pound Recipe (12 slices)		2-Pound Recipe (16 slices)
3/4 cup plus 2 tablespoons	Water	1 cup plus 2 tablespoons
1/4 cup	Orange juice	1/3 cup
2 tablespoons	Honey	2 tablespoons
1 teaspoon	Grated orange peel	1 1/2 teaspoons
2 tablespoons	Margarine or butter, softened	2 tablespoons
3 cups	Bread flour	4 cups
1/2 cup	Old-fashioned or quick-cooking oats	2/3 cup
1/3 cup	Cornmeal	1/2 cup
1 1/4 teaspoons	Salt	1 1/4 teaspoons
2 1/2 teaspoons	Bread machine or quick active dry yeast	2 3/4 teaspoons

Make 1 1/2-Pound Recipe with bread machines that use 3 cups flour, or make 2-Pound Recipe with bread machines that use 4 cups flour.

Measure carefully, placing all ingredients in bread machine pan in the order recommended by the manufacturer.

Select Basic/White cycle. Use Medium or Light crust color. Do not use delay cycles. Remove baked bread from pan, and cool on wire rack.

■ 1 Slice: 180 calories (25 calories from fat); 3g fat (1g saturated); 0mg cholesterol; 270mg sodium; 35g carbohydrate (2g dietary fiber); 5g protein

TRY THIS

Making stuffing for dinner? The combination of oats and cornmeal with the hint of orange makes this a good bread to use for your favorite stuffing recipe. Try adding some pecan halves, raisins or dried cranberries or cherries. It's great with chicken and turkey and for stuffing pork chops.

DID YOU KNOW?

Cornmeal can be yellow, white or blue, depending on the type of corn from which it is made. Yellow cornmeal has slightly more vitamin A than white cornmeal. We like yellow cornmeal for this bread because it adds a sunny color that goes so well with the flavor of the orange juice. You may want to try the recipe with white or blue cornmeal for a change.

Granola Bread

We found from our testing that for good texture and volume, slightly less yeast is needed in the 2-pound loaf than is needed in the 1 1/2-pound loaf.

DID YOU KNOW?

Granola is a mixture of various grains but is usually made of oats, and it can include nuts and dried fruits. Use your favorite when making this bread. Some purchased granolas are toasted with oil and honey, which makes them crispier and slightly sweeter.

1 1/2-Pound Recipe (12 slices)		2-Pound Recipe (16 slices)
1 1/4 cups	Water	1 3/4 cups
2 tablespoons	Margarine or butter, softened	2 tablespoons
2 tablespoons	Packed brown sugar	2 tablespoons
3 cups	Bread flour	4 1/4 cups
3/4 cup	Granola (any flavor)	1 cup
2 tablespoons	Dry milk	2 tablespoons
1 teaspoon	Salt	1 1/2 teaspoons
1 1/2 teaspoons	Bread machine or quick active dry yeast	1 1/4 teaspoons

Make 1 1/2-Pound Recipe with bread machines that use 3 cups flour, or make 2-Pound Recipe with bread machines that use at least 4 cups flour.

Measure carefully, placing all ingredients in bread machine pan in the order recommended by the manufacturer.

Select Basic/White cycle. Use Medium or Light crust color. Remove baked bread from pan, and cool on wire rack.

■ 1 Slice: 185 calories (35 calories from fat); 4g fat (2g saturated); 0mg cholesterol; 220mg sodium; 33g carbohydrate (1g dietary fiber); 5g protein

Granola Bread

Cranberry Corn Bread

SUCCESS TIP

We found from our testing that the same amount of yeast is needed for both the 1 1/2-pound and 2-pound loaves.

SUCCESS TIP

If your bread machine doesn't have a Raisin/Nut signal, add the cranberries 5 to 10 minutes before the last kneading cycle ends. Check your bread machine's use-and-care book to find out how long the last cycle runs.

TRY THIS

For a slightly sweeter bread, use the same amount of honey instead of the molasses.

1 1/2-Pound Recipe (12 slices)		2-Pound Recipe (16 slices)
1 cup plus 1 tablespoon	Water	1 1/4 cups
3 tablespoons	Molasses	3 tablespoons
2 tablespoons	Margarine or butter, softened	2 tablespoons
3 cups	Bread flour	4 cups
1/3 cup	Cornmeal	1/2 cup
1 1/2 teaspoons	Salt	1 1/2 teaspoons
2 teaspoons	Bread machine or quick active dry yeast	2 teaspoons
1/2 cup	Dried cranberries	2/3 cup

Make 1 1/2-Pound Recipe with bread machines that use 3 cups flour, or make 2-Pound Recipe with bread machines that use 4 cups flour.

Measure carefully, placing all ingredients except cranberries in bread machine pan in the order recommended by the manufacturer. Add cranberries at the Raisin/Nut signal.

Select Basic/White cycle. Use Medium or Light crust color. Do not use delay cycles if using honey. Remove baked bread from pan, and cool on wire rack.

■ 1 Slice: 175 calories (20 calories from fat); 2g fat (0g saturated); 0mg cholesterol; 320mg sodium; 38g carbohydrate (3g dietary fiber); 4g protein

Honey Corn Bread

1 1/2-Pound Recipe (12 slices)		2-Pound Recipe (16 slices)
1 egg plus enough water to equal 1 cup	Egg	1 egg plus enough water to equal 1 1/3 cups
1/3 cup	Honey	1/2 cup
3 tablespoons	Margarine or butter, softened	1/4 cup
3 cups	Bread flour	4 cups
1/2 cup	Cornmeal	2/3 cup
2 tablespoons	Dry milk	3 tablespoons
1 teaspoon	Salt	2 teaspoons
1 1/4 teaspoons	Bread machine or quick active dry yeast	1 1/2 teaspoons

Make 1 1/2-Pound Recipe with bread machines that use 3 cups flour, or make 2-Pound Recipe with bread machines that use 4 cups flour.

Measure carefully, placing all ingredients in bread machine pan in the order recommended by the manufacturer.

Select Basic/White cycle. Use Medium or Light crust color. Do not use delay cycles. Remove baked bread from pan, and cool on wire rack.

■ 1 Slice: 210 calories (35 calories from fat); 4g fat (1g saturated); 20mg cholesterol; 220mg sodium; 39g carbohydrate (1g dietary fiber); 5g protein

TRY THIS

The cornmeal adds a nice texture to this loaf, which also means it's a perfect choice for homemade croutons. Toss them in your favorite salad, or use to top off tomato or cheese soup. This bread also makes good fresh bread crumbs to sprinkle on casseroles before baking for added texture and flavor.

SANDWICH BOARD

Enjoy a Prosciutto and Brie Sandwich with a tall glass of iced tea on your deck or porch. Spread orange marmalade on two slices of bread, and sprinkle with finely chopped toasted pecans or walnuts. Layer one slice with thin slices of prosciutto or ham and Brie cheese. Top with watercress or spinach and remaining slice of bread.

Fruit and Veggie Harvest Loaves

Sweet Orange Bread (page 102)

Caramel Apple and Pecan Bread

1 1/2-Pound Recipe (12 slices)		2-Pound Recipe (16 slices)
1 cup	Water	1 1/4 cups
2 tablespoons	Margarine or butter, softened	2 tablespoons
3 cups	Bread flour	4 cups
1/4 cup	Packed brown sugar	1/3 cup
3/4 teaspoon	Ground cinnamon	3/4 teaspoon
1 teaspoon	Salt	1 1/4 teaspoons
2 teaspoons	Bread machine or quick active dry yeast	2 teaspoons
1/2 cup	Chopped unpeeled apple	2/3 cup
1/3 cup	Coarsely chopped pecans, toasted (page 194)	1/2 cup

Make 1 1/2-Pound Recipe with bread machines that use 3 cups flour, or make 2-Pound Recipe with bread machines that use 4 cups flour.

Measure carefully, placing all ingredients except apple and pecans in bread machine pan in the order recommended by the manufacturer. Add apple and pecans at the Raisin/Nut signal.

Select Sweet or Basic/White cycle. Use Light crust color. Do not use delay cycles. Remove baked bread from pan, and cool on wire rack.

■ 1 Slice: 185 calories (45 calories from fat); 5g fat (1g saturated); 0mg cholesterol; 220mg sodium; 32g carbohydrate (1g dietary fiber); 4g protein

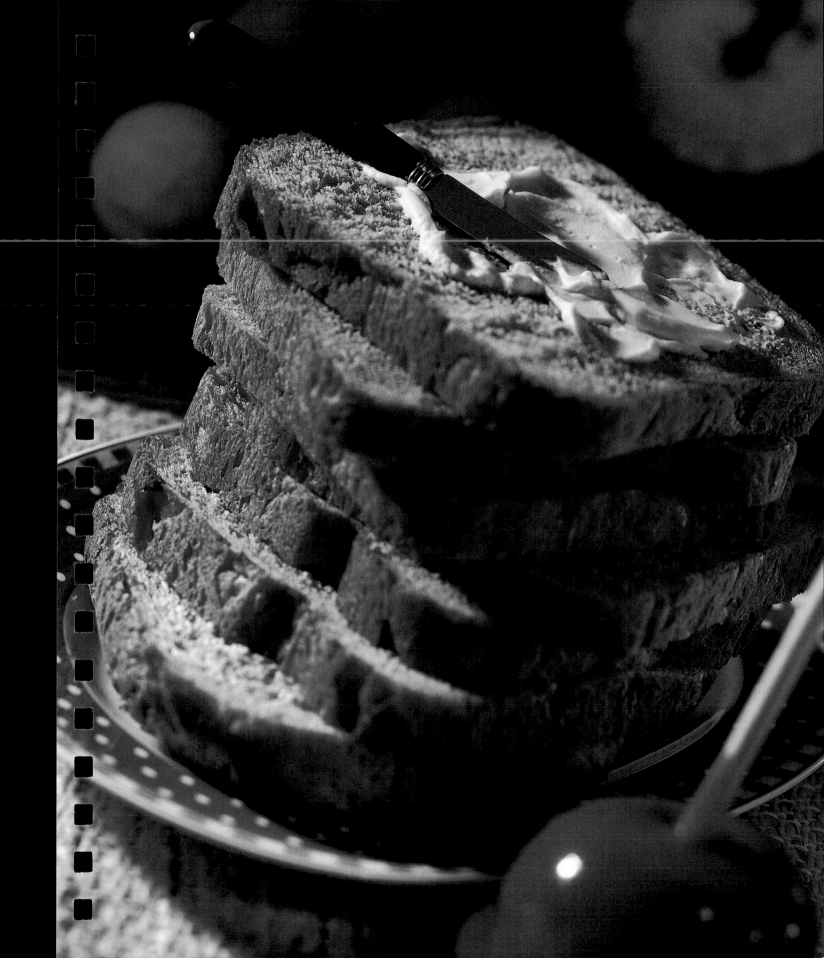

Orange Applesauce Bread

SUCCESS TIP

We found from our testing that the same amount of yeast is needed for both the 1 1/2-pound and 2-pound loaves.

DID YOU KNOW?

Wheat germ, which is the embryo of the wheat berry, is a good source of vitamins, minerals and protein. It also adds a nice nutty flavor to this applesauce bread. Wheat germ contains oil, so it can turn rancid quickly if not stored properly. After it is opened, keep it in the refrigerator, and be sure to taste it before adding it to the recipe.

1 1/2-Pound Recipe (12 slices)		2-Pound Recipe (16 slices)
1/2 cup	Apple juice	1/2 cup plus 1 tablespoon
1/4 cup	Water	1/3 cup
1/3 cup	Unsweetened applesauce	1/2 cup
2 tablespoons	Margarine or butter, softened	2 tablespoons
1 teaspoon	Grated orange peel	1 1/4 teaspoons
3 cups	Bread flour	4 cups
2 tablespoons	Wheat germ	3 tablespoons
2 tablespoons	Dry milk	2 tablespoons
1/4 cup	Sugar	1/3 cup
1 1/4 teaspoons	Salt	1 1/2 teaspoons
2 teaspoons	Bread machine yeast or quick active dry yeast	2 teaspoons

Make 1 1/2-Pound Recipe with bread machines that use 3 cups flour, or make 2-Pound Recipe with bread machines that use 4 cups flour.

Measure carefully, placing all ingredients in bread machine pan in the order recommended by the manufacturer.

Select Sweet or Basic/White cycle. Use Light or Medium crust color. Do not use delay cycles. Remove baked bread from pan, and cool on wire rack.

■ 1 Slice: 170 calories (20 calories from fat); 2g fat (0g saturated); 0mg cholesterol; 280mg sodium; 34g carbohydrate (1g dietary fiber); 5g protein

Orange Applesauce Bread

Dried Apricot Bread

SUCCESS TIP

We found from our testing that the same amount of yeast is needed for both the 1 1/2-pound and 2-pound loaves.

SUCCESS TIP

If your bread machine doesn't have a Raisin/Nut signal, add the apricots 5 to 10 minutes before the last kneading cycle ends. Check your bread machine's use-and-care book to find out how long the last cycle runs.

SUCCESS TIP

Sugar helps to brown the crust of baked foods. Because dried apricots have a high amount of sugar, we recommend using a medium or light crust setting so the crust doesn't become too dark during baking.

1 1/2-Pound Recipe (12 slices)		2-Pound Recipe (16 slices)
1 cup plus 1 tablespoon	Water	1 1/4 cups
1 tablespoon	Margarine or butter, softened	2 tablespoons
3 cups	Bread flour	4 cups
1 tablespoon	Sugar	1 tablespoon
1/2 teaspoon	Ground nutmeg	3/4 teaspoon
1 1/2 teaspoons	Salt	1 3/4 teaspoons
2 1/4 teaspoons	Bread machine or quick active dry yeast	2 1/4 teaspoons
2/3 cup	Dried apricots, cut into fourths	3/4 cup

Make 1 1/2-Pound Recipe with bread machines that use 3 cups flour, or make 2-Pound Recipe with bread machines that use 4 cups flour.

Measure carefully, placing all ingredients except apricots in bread machine pan in the order recommended by the manufacturer. Add apricots at the Raisin/Nut signal.

Select Basic/White cycle. Use Medium or Light crust color. Remove baked bread from pan, and cool on wire rack.

■ 1 Slice: 135 calories (10 calories from fat); 1g fat (0g saturated); 0mg cholesterol; 300mg sodium; 32g carbohydrate (2g dietary fiber); 4g protein

Banana Caramel Bread

1 1/2-Pound Recipe (12 slices)		2-Pound Recipe (16 slices)
3/4 cup plus 2 tablespoons	Water	1 cup plus 2 tablespoons
1/3 cup	Caramel topping	1/3 cup
2 tablespoons	Margarine or butter, softened	2 tablespoons
3 cups	Bread flour	3 3/4 cups
2 tablespoons	Dry milk	2 tablespoons
2 tablespoons	Sugar	3 tablespoons
1 1/4 teaspoons	Salt	1 1/4 teaspoons
2 1/2 teaspoons	Bread machine or quick active dry yeast	2 1/2 teaspoons
2/3 cup	Dried banana chips	3/4 cup

Make 1 1/2-Pound Recipe with bread machines that use 3 cups flour, or make 2-Pound Recipe with bread machines that use 4 cups flour.

Measure carefully, placing all ingredients except banana chips in bread machine pan in the order recommended by the manufacturer. Add banana chips at the Raisin/Nut signal.

Select Sweet or Basic/White cycle. Use Light crust color. Do not use delay cycles. Remove baked bread from pan, and cool on wire rack.

■ 1 Slice: 200 calories (35 calories from fat); 4g fat (2g saturated); 0mg cholesterol; 300mg sodium; 38g carbohydrate (1g dietary fiber); 4g protein

SUCCESS TIP

If your bread machine doesn't have a Raisin/Nut signal, add the banana chips 5 to 10 minutes before the last kneading cycle ends. Check your bread machine's use-and-care book to find out how long the last cycle runs.

SUCCESS TIP

We found from our testing that the same amount of yeast is needed for both the 1 1/2-pound and 2-pound loaves.

SUCCESS TIP

Use the light crust setting so that the crust won't become too dark brown from the sugar in the caramel topping and dried bananas.

SANDWICH BOARD

Want to give the kids a special treat? Make their next peanut butter and jelly sandwich with this yummy banana-flavored bread. Or use only peanut butter and cook it just like a grilled cheese sandwich.

Raisin Banana Bread

SUCCESS TIP

If your bread machine doesn't have a Raisin/Nut signal, add the raisins 5 to 10 minutes before the last kneading cycle ends. Check your bread machine's use-and-care book to find out how long the last cycle runs.

SUCCESS TIP

We found from our testing that the same amount of yeast is needed for both the 1 1/2-pound and 2-pound loaves.

DID YOU KNOW?

If you have too many overripe bananas, pop them into the freezer in their peels until you are ready to bake. Let them stand at room temperature until they are thawed, then peel and mash.

1 1/2-Pound Recipe (12 slices)		2-Pound Recipe (16 slices)
3/4 cup plus 2 tablespoons	Water	1 cup
3 cups	Bread flour	4 cups
1/2 cup	Mashed banana(s)	2/3 cup
2 tablespoons	Packed brown sugar	2 tablespoons
1 1/2 teaspoons	Salt	2 teaspoons
1 teaspoon	Ground cinnamon	1 teaspoon
2 teaspoons	Bread machine or quick active dry yeast	2 teaspoons
1/2 cup	Raisins	2/3 cup
	Cinnamon Glaze (below), if desired	

Make 1 1/2-Pound Recipe with bread machines that use 3 cups flour, or make 2-Pound Recipe with bread machines that use 4 cups flour.

Measure carefully, placing all ingredients except raisins and Cinnamon Glaze in bread machine pan in the order recommended by the manufacturer. Add raisins at the Raisin/Nut signal.

Select Sweet or Basic/White cycle. Use Medium or Light crust color. Do not use delay cycles. Remove baked bread from pan, and cool on wire rack. Drizzle with Cinnamon Glaze.

Cinnamon Glaze

1/2 cup powdered sugar

1 to 2 teaspoons milk

Dash of ground cinnamon

Mix all ingredients until smooth and thin enough to drizzle.

■ 1 Slice: 150 calories (0 calories from fat); 0g fat (0g saturated); 0mg cholesterol; 270mg sodium; 36g carbohydrate (2g dietary fiber); 4g protein

Double-Cherry Pecan Bread

1 1/2-Pound Recipe (12 slices)		2-Pound Recipe (16 slices)
1 cup plus 1 tablespoon	Cherry-flavored fruit drink	1 1/3 cups
1 teaspoon	Salt	1 1/2 teaspoons
2 tablespoons	Sugar	1/3 cup
1 tablespoon	Margarine or butter, softened	2 tablespoons
1 1/2 teaspoons	Vanilla	2 teaspoons
3 1/4 cups	Bread flour	4 1/4 cups
1 tablespoon plus 1 1/2 teaspoons	Dry milk	2 tablespoons
1/3 cup	Dried cherries	1/2 cup
1/2 cup	Pecan halves	2/3 cup
1 teaspoon	Bread machine or quick active dry yeast	1 teaspoon

SUCCESS TIP

We found from our testing that the same amount of yeast is needed for both the 1 1/2-pound and 2-pound loaves.

Make 1 1/2-Pound Recipe with bread machines that use at least 3 cups flour, or make 2-Pound Recipe with bread machines that use at least 4 cups flour.

Measure carefully, placing all ingredients in bread machine pan in the order recommended by the manufacturer.

TRY THIS

For a bread that will complement any fall dinner, use a cranberry-flavored fruit drink, dried cranberries and walnut halves.

Select Sweet or Basic/White cycle. Use Medium or Light crust color. Remove baked bread from pan, and cool on wire rack.

■ 1 Slice: 190 calories (35 calories from fat); 4g fat (1g saturated); 0mg cholesterol; 200mg sodium; 36g carbohydrate (2g dietary fiber); 5g protein

Cranberry Blueberry Bread

SUCCESS TIP

If your bread machine doesn't have a Raisin/Nut signal, add the cranberries and blueberries 5 to 10 minutes before the last kneading cycle ends. Check your bread machine's use-and-care book to find out how long the last cycle runs.

SUCCESS TIP

We found from our testing that the same amount of yeast is needed for both the 1 1/2-pound and 2-pound loaves.

TRY THIS

Dried cherries are a nice replacement for the dried cranberries for a red, white and blue loaf of summer bread.

1 1/2-Pound Recipe (12 slices)		2-Pound Recipe (16 slices)
1 cup plus 1 tablespoon	Water	1 cup plus 3 tablespoons
3 tablespoons	Honey	1/4 cup
2 tablespoons	Margarine or butter, softened	2 tablespoons
3 cups	Bread flour	4 cups
1 1/4 teaspoons	Salt	1 1/2 teaspoons
2 teaspoons	Bread machine or quick active dry yeast	2 teaspoons
1/4 cup	Dried cranberries	1/3 cup
1/4 cup	Dried blueberries	1/3 cup

Make 1 1/2-Pound Recipe with bread machines that use 3 cups flour, or make 2-Pound Recipe with bread machines that use 4 cups flour.

Measure carefully, placing all ingredients except cranberries and blueberries in bread machine pan in the order recommended by the manufacturer. Add cranberries and blueberries at the Raisin/Nut signal.

Select Sweet or Basic/White cycle. Use Medium or Light crust color. Do not use delay cycles. Remove baked bread from pan, and cool on wire rack.

■ 1 Slice: 165 calories (20 calories from fat); 2g fat (0g saturated); 0mg cholesterol; 270mg sodium; 35g carbohydrate (2g dietary fiber); 4g protein

Cranberry Blueberry Bread

Sweet Orange Bread

SUCCESS TIP

We found from our testing that for good texture and volume, slightly less yeast is needed in the 2-pound loaf than is needed in the 1 1/2-pound loaf.

SUCCESS TIP

Dividing a raw egg in half isn't easy! To do it, slightly beat the egg with a fork or wire whisk just until it is mixed. Then measure 2 tablespoons of the beaten egg, which is equal to half a large egg.

1 1/2-Pound Recipe (12 slices)		2-Pound Recipe (16 slices)
3/4 cup minus 3 tablespoons	Water	3/4 cup
3 tablespoons	Frozen orange juice concentrate, thawed	1/4 cup
1 1/2	Eggs (See Success Tip)	2
3 cups	Bread flour	4 cups
1/2 teaspoon	Grated orange peel	1/2 teaspoon
1/4 cup	Sugar	1/4 cup
2 tablespoons	Dry milk	3 tablespoons
1 1/2 tablespoons	Margarine or butter, softened	2 tablespoons
1 1/4 teaspoons	Salt	1 1/2 teaspoons
2 teaspoons	Bread machine or quick active dry yeast	1 1/2 teaspoons
	Orange Glaze (below), if desired	

Make 1 1/2-Pound Recipe with bread machines that use 3 cups flour, or make 2-Pound Recipe with bread machines that use 4 cups flour.

Measure carefully, placing all ingredients except Orange Glaze in bread machine pan in the order recommended by the manufacturer.

Select Sweet or Basic/White cycle. Use Medium or Light crust color. Do not use delay cycles. Remove baked bread from pan, and cool on wire rack. Drizzle with Orange Glaze.

Orange Glaze

1/2 cup powdered sugar

1/8 teaspoon grated orange peel, if desired

1 to 2 teaspoons orange juice

Mix all ingredients until smooth and thin enough to drizzle.

■ 1 Slice: 165 calories (20 calories from fat); 2g fat (0g saturated); 25mg cholesterol; 250mg sodium; 33g carbohydrate (1g dietary fiber); 5g protein

Peach Maple Bread

1 1/2-Pound Recipe (12 slices)		2-Pound Recipe (16 slices)
3/4 cup plus 2 tablespoons	Water	1 cup
1/4 cup	Maple-flavored syrup	1/3 cup
1 tablespoon	Margarine or butter, softened	1 tablespoon
3 cups	Bread flour	3 2/3 cups
2 tablespoons	Packed brown sugar	2 tablespoons
1/4 teaspoon	Ground nutmeg	1/2 teaspoon
1 1/4 teaspoons	Salt	1 1/4 teaspoons
2 1/4 teaspoons	Bread machine or quick active dry yeast	2 1/2 teaspoons
1/2 cup	Cut-up dried peaches	2/3 cup

Make 1 1/2-Pound Recipe with bread machines that use 3 cups flour, or make 2-Pound Recipe with bread machines that use 4 cups flour.

Measure carefully, placing all ingredients except peaches in bread machine pan in the order recommended by the manufacturer. Add peaches at the Raisin/Nut signal.

Select Sweet or Basic/White cycle. Use Light crust color. Remove baked bread from pan, and cool on wire rack.

■ 1 Slice: 170 calories (10 calories from fat); 1g fat (0g saturated); 0mg cholesterol; 260mg sodium; 37g carbohydrate (1g dietary fiber); 4g protein

SUCCESS TIP

If your bread machine doesn't have a Raisin/Nut signal, add the peaches 5 to 10 minutes before the last kneading cycle ends. Check your bread machine's use and care book to find out how long the last cycle runs.

TRY THIS

Can't find dried peaches? Dried apricots also would taste good in this bread since their flavor goes so well with the hint of maple flavoring and nutmeg found in this bread.

Brandied Pumpkin Bread

SUCCESS TIP

If your bread machine has a pan capacity of 9 to 12 cups, you will need to decrease the yeast to 1 3/4 teaspoons for the 1 1/2-pound loaf, so the bread won't touch the lid of the bread machine during baking.

SUCCESS TIP

We found from our testing that for good texture and volume, slightly less yeast is needed in the 2-pound loaf than is needed in the 1 1/2-pound loaf.

SUCCESS TIP

Check the label on your can of pumpkin to be sure it is solid-pack pumpkin and that pumpkin is the only ingredient. Canned pumpkin pie filling has other ingredients and seasonings added and is not appropriate for this recipe.

TRY THIS

No pumpkin pie spice on your cupboard shelf? Mix 1/2 teaspoon ground cinnamon, 1/4 teaspoon ground ginger, 1/8 teaspoon ground allspice and 1/8 teaspoon ground nutmeg, and you will have a teaspoon of your own pumpkin pie spice.

1 1/2-Pound Recipe (12 slices)		2-Pound Recipe (16 slices)
3/4 cup	Canned pumpkin	1 cup
1/2 cup	Water	1/2 cup plus 2 tablespoons
1/2 teaspoon	Brandy extract or vanilla	3/4 teaspoon
2 tablespoons	Margarine or butter, softened	2 tablespoons
3 cups	Bread flour	4 cups
1/4 cup	Sugar	1/3 cup
1 1/4 teaspoons	Salt	1 1/4 teaspoons
1/2 teaspoon	Pumpkin pie spice	1/2 teaspoon
2 1/4 teaspoons	Bread machine or quick active dry yeast	1 3/4 teaspoons

Make 1 1/2-Pound Recipe with bread machines that use 3 cups flour, or make 2-Pound Recipe with bread machines that use 4 cups flour.

Measure carefully, placing all ingredients in bread machine pan in the order recommended by the manufacturer.

Select Sweet or Basic/White cycle. Use Light crust color. Do not use delay cycles. Remove baked bread from pan, and cool on wire rack.

1 Slice: 160 calories (20 calories from fat); 2g fat (0g saturated); 0mg cholesterol; 270mg sodium; 32g carbohydrate (1g dietary fiber); 4g protein

Panettone

1 1/2-Pound Recipe (12 slices)		2-Pound Recipe (16 slices)
3/4 cup plus 2 tablespoons	Milk	1 1/3 cups
1	Egg	1
2 tablespoons	Margarine or butter, softened	3 tablespoons
1 teaspoon	Salt	1 1/2 teaspoons
3 cups	Bread flour	4 cups
1 1/2 teaspoons	Anise seed, crushed	2 teaspoons
2 teaspoons	Bread machine or quick active dry yeast	2 teaspoons
1/3 cup	Coarsely chopped dried or candied pineapple	1/2 cup
1/3 cup	Chopped candied citron, drained	1/2 cup

Make 1 1/2-Pound Recipe with bread machines that use 3 cups flour, or make 2-Pound Recipe with bread machines that use 4 cups flour.

Measure carefully, placing all ingredients except pineapple and citron in bread machine pan in the order recommended by the manufacturer. Add pineapple and citron at the Raisin/Nut signal.

Select Basic/White cycle. Use Medium or Light crust color. Do not use delay cycles. Remove baked bread from pan, and cool on wire rack.

■ 1 Slice: 170 calories (25 calories from fat); 3g fat (1g saturated); 20mg cholesterol; 250mg sodium; 33g carbohydrate (2g dietary fiber); 5g protein

SUCCESS TIP

We found from our testing that the same amount of yeast is needed for both the 1 1/2-pound and 2-pound loaves.

SUCCESS TIP

If your bread machine doesn't have a Raisin/Nut signal, add the pineapple and citron 5 to 10 minutes before the last kneading cycle ends. Check your bread machine's use-and-care book to find out how long the last cycle runs.

DID YOU KNOW?

Panettone (pronounced pan-uh-TOH-nee) is a sweet yeast bread that originated in Milan, Italy. Since it is made in a tall cylindrical shape, the vertical bread machine pan is perfect for this bread. Panettone is traditionally served at Christmastime but also at other celebrations such as weddings and christenings. This bread makes a great holiday gift, wrapped in clear cellophane and tied with a big red bow, just as they do in Italy.

Caramelized Onion Bread

SUCCESS TIP

If your bread machine doesn't have a Raisin/Nut signal, add the caramelized onions 5 to 10 minutes before the last kneading cycle ends. Check your bread machine's use-and-care book to find out how long the last cycle runs.

SUCCESS TIP

The onions need to cook slowly, so the natural sugar in them can caramelize and develop that delicious delicate sweet flavor. So be patient, and don't increase the heat to make the onions brown more quickly.

1 1/2-Pound Recipe (12 slices)		2-Pound Recipe (16 slices)
1/2 cup	Caramelized Onions (below)	2/3 cup
1 cup	Water	1 1/4 cups
1 tablespoon	Olive or vegetable oil	1 tablespoon
3 cups	Bread flour	4 cups
2 tablespoons	Sugar	2 tablespoons
1 teaspoon	Salt	1 teaspoon
1/4 teaspoons	Bread machine or quick active dry yeast	1 1/2 teaspoons

Make 1 1/2-Pound Recipe with bread machines that use 3 cups flour, or make 2-pound Recipe with bread machines that use 4 cups flour.

Prepare Caramelized Onions.

Measure carefully, placing all ingredients except onions in bread machine pan in the order recommended by the manufacturer. Add onions at the Raisin/Nut signal.

Select Basic/White cycle. Use Medium or Light crust color. Do not use delay cycles. Remove baked bread from pan, and cool on wire rack.

Caramelized Onions

1 tablespoon margarine or butter

2 medium onions, sliced

Melt margarine in 10-inch skillet over medium-low heat. Cook onions in margarine 10 to 15 minutes, stirring occasionally, until onions are brown and caramelized; remove from heat.

■ 1 Slice: 150 calories (10 calories from fat); 1g fat (1g saturated); 0mg cholesterol; 320mg sodium; 31g carbohydrate (1g dietary fiber); 5g protein

Caramelized Onion Bread

Spinach Cheese Bread

SUCCESS TIP

Use only fresh spinach for this cheesy bread because frozen or canned spinach has too much water, which will cause the loaf to become gummy.

SUCCESS TIP

If your bread machine doesn't have a Raisin/Nut signal, add the spinach 5 to 10 minutes before the last kneading cycle ends. Check your bread machine's use-and-care book to find out how long the last cycle runs.

SANDWICH BOARD

Need a little something to serve with a bowl of soup or a large salad? These Bell Pepper and Cheese Triangles are the perfect answer. Top slices of this bread with sliced Cheddar cheese and finely chopped red and green bell peppers. Broil bread with tops 4 to 6 inches from heat 1 to 2 minutes or until cheese is melted. Cut each slice on the diagonal into triangles.

1 1/2-Pound Recipe (12 slices)		2-Pound Recipe (16 slices)
3/4 cup plus 2 tablespoons	Water	1 1/4 cups
3 cups	Bread flour	4 cups
3/4 cup	Shredded sharp Cheddar cheese	1 cup
1/4 cup	Grated Parmesan cheese	1/3 cup
2 teaspoons	Instant minced onion	1 tablespoon
1 tablespoon	Sugar	4 teaspoons
3/4 teaspoon	Salt	1 teaspoon
1 1/4 teaspoons	Bread machine or quick active dry yeast	1 3/4 teaspoons
3/4 cup	Chopped fresh spinach leaves	1 cup

Make 1 1/2-Pound Recipe with bread machines that use 3 cups flour, or make 2-Pound Recipe with bread machines that use 4 cups flour.

Measure carefully, placing all ingredients except spinach in bread machine pan in the order recommended by the manufacturer. Add spinach at the Raisin/Nut signal.

Select Basic/White cycle. Use Medium or Light crust color. Do not use delay cycles. Remove baked bread from pan, and cool on wire rack.

■ 1 Slice: 160 calories (25 calories from fat); 3g fat (2g saturated); 10mg cholesterol; 220mg sodium; 28g carbohydrate (1g dietary fiber); 6g protein

Spinach Cheese Bread

Double-Garlic Potato Bread

SUCCESS TIP

We found from our testing that for good texture and volume, slightly less yeast is needed in the 2-pound loaf than is needed in the 1 1/2-pound loaf.

TRY THIS

If you don't have the roasted garlic mashed potato mix, use the same amount of unflavored mashed potato mix and increase the garlic powder to 1/2 teaspoon.

SANDWICH BOARD

The garlic in this bread adds a nice flavor to Grilled Fontina and Roasted Peppers. Spread your favorite mustard on two slices of bread. Layer one slice with Fontina cheese and roasted red bell peppers; top with the remaining slice. Butter the outside of the sandwich, then cook over medium heat until it's golden brown and the cheese is melted, which will take about 8 minutes.

1 1/2-Pound Recipe (12 slices)		2-Pound Recipe (16 slices)
1 cup	Water	1 1/4 cups
2 tablespoons	Margarine or butter, softened	3 tablespoons
1	Egg	1
3 cups	Bread flour	4 cups
2/3 cup	Mashed potato mix seasoned with roasted garlic (dry)	2/3 cup
1 tablespoon	Sugar	1 tablespoon
1 1/2 teaspoons	Salt	1 1/2 teaspoons
1/4 teaspoon	Garlic powder	1/4 teaspoon
2 1/2 teaspoons	Bread machine or quick active dry yeast	2 teaspoons

Make 1 1/2-Pound Recipe with bread machines that use 3 cups flour, or make 2-Pound Recipe with bread machines that use 4 cups flour.

Measure carefully, placing all ingredients in bread machine pan in the order recommended by the manufacturer.

Select Basic/White cycle. Use Medium or Light crust color. Do not use delay cycles. Remove baked bread from pan, and cool on wire rack.

■ 1 Slice: 150 calories (20 calories from fat); 2g fat (0g saturated); 0mg cholesterol; 320mg sodium; 30g carbohydrate (1g dietary fiber); 4g protein

Double-Garlic Potato Bread

Peppery Potato and Carrot Bread

SUCCESS TIP

Most graters have two sizes of shredders—one for small shreds and one for medium size. Be sure to use the medium-size shred for the carrots. If you use the small shred, you may have too much carrot, which will cause the dough to be too moist.

SANDWICH BOARD

Make your next grilled cheese a Roasted Garlic Grilled Cheese on this Peppery Potato and Carrot Bread. Make the Roasted Garlic on page 34. Spread the garlic on two slices of bread. Layer one slice of bread with slices of Monterey Jack, Muenster or provolone cheese; top with the remaining slice of bread. If you like, add some sliced avocado. Butter the outside of the sandwich, then cook over medium heat until it's golden brown and the cheese is melted, which will take about 8 minutes.

1 1/2-Pound Recipe (12 slices)		2-Pound Recipe (16 slices)
1 cup plus 2 tablespoons	Water	1 1/4 cups
2/3 cup	Shredded carrots	2/3 cup
2 tablespoons	Margarine or butter, softened	2 tablespoons
3 cups	Bread flour	4 cups
1/2 cup	Mashed potato mix (dry)	1/2 cup
1 teaspoon	Lemon pepper seasoning salt	1 1/4 teaspoons
1 tablespoon	Sugar	2 tablespoons
1 teaspoon	Salt	1 1/4 teaspoons
1 1/2 teaspoons	Bread machine or quick active dry yeast	1 3/4 teaspoons

Make 1 1/2-Pound Recipe with bread machines that use 3 cups flour, or make 2-Pound Recipe with bread machines that use 4 cups flour.

Measure carefully, placing all ingredients in bread machine pan in the order recommended by the manufacturer.

Select Basic/White cycle. Use Medium or Light crust color. Do not use delay cycles. Remove baked bread from pan, and cool on wire rack.

■ 1 Slice: 150 calories (20 calories from fat); 2g fat (1g saturated); 0mg cholesterol; 250mg sodium; 30g carbohydrate (1g dietary fiber); 4g protein

Peppery Potato and Carrot Bread

Maple Sweet Potato Bread

SUCCESS TIP

We found from our testing that for good texture and volume, slightly less yeast is needed in the 2-pound loaf than is needed in the 1 1/2-pound loaf.

SUCCESS TIP

Be sure to use vacuum-pack sweet potatoes because they are drier than regular canned sweet potatoes. The extra liquid in the regular canned sweet potatoes makes the dough too moist, which will cause the loaf to be gummy and possibly make the loaf collapse after baking.

1 1/2-Pound Recipe (12 slices)		2-Pound Recipe (16 slices)
3/4 cup	Canned vacuum-pack sweet potatoes, drained and mashed	1 cup
1/2 cup	Water	1/2 cup plus 1 tablespoon
3 tablespoons	Sour cream	3 tablespoons
1 teaspoon	Maple extract	1 1/4 teaspoons
3 cups	Bread flour	4 cups
1/4 cup	Sugar	1/3 cup
1/2 teaspoon	Ground cinnamon	3/4 teaspoon
1 teaspoon	Salt	1 1/4 teaspoons
2 teaspoons	Bread machine or quick active dry yeast	1 3/4 teaspoons

Make 1 1/2-Pound Recipe with bread machines that use 3 cups flour, or make 2-Pound Recipe with bread machines that use 4 cups flour.

Measure carefully, placing all ingredients in bread machine pan in the order recommended by the manufacturer.

Select Sweet or Basic/White cycle. Use Medium or Light crust color. Do not use delay cycles. Remove baked bread from pan, and cool on wire rack.

■ 1 Slice: 155 calories (10 calories from fat); 1g fat (1g saturated); 5mg cholesterol; 210mg sodium; 33g carbohydrate (1g dietary fiber); 4g protein

Maple Sweet Potato Bread

Dilled Carrot Bread

SUCCESS TIP

We found from our testing that for good texture and volume, slightly less yeast is needed in the 2-pound loaf than is needed in the 1 1/2-pound loaf.

TRY THIS

For a hint of the Mediterranean in this golden carrot bread, use the same amount of fennel seed instead of the dill weed.

1 1/2-Pound Recipe (12 slices)		2-Pound Recipe (16 slices)
1 cup plus 2 tablespoons	Water	1 1/3 cups
1/2 cup	Shredded carrots	2/3 cup
2 tablespoons	Margarine or butter, softened	2 tablespoons
2 tablespoons	Sugar	2 tablespoons
3 cups	Bread flour	4 1/4 cups
1 cup	Fiber One ® cereal	1 1/3 cups
1 1/2 teaspoons	Dried dill weed	2 teaspoons
1 teaspoon	Salt	1 1/2 teaspoons
1 1/2 teaspoons	Bread machine or quick active dry yeast	1 1/4 teaspoons

Make 1 1/2-Pound Recipe with bread machines that use 3 cups flour, or make 2-Pound Recipe with bread machines that use at least 4 cups flour.

Measure carefully, placing all ingredients in bread machine pan in the order recommended by the manufacturer.

Select Basic/White cycle. Use Medium or Light crust color. Do not use delay cycles. Remove baked bread from pan, and cool on wire rack.

■ 1 Slice: 165 calories (25 calories from fat); 3g fat (0g saturated); 0mg cholesterol; 230mg sodium; 33g carbohydrate (3g dietary fiber); 4g protein

Potato Tarragon Bread

SUCCESS TIP

We found from our testing that for good texture and volume, less yeast is needed in the 2-pound loaf than is needed in the 1 1/2-pound loaf.

TRY THIS

For a delicious Potato Chive Bread, use the same amount of freeze-dried chives or 1 tablespoon chopped fresh chives for the tarragon.

1 1/2-Pound Recipe (12 slices)		2-Pound Recipe (16 slices)
1 cup	Water	1 1/3 cups
3 tablespoons	Margarine or butter, softened	1/4 cup
1	Egg(s)	2
3 cups	Bread flour	4 cups
3/4 cup	Mashed potato mix (dry)	1 cup
1 tablespoon	Sugar	1 tablespoon
1 1/2 teaspoons	Salt	2 teaspoons
1 1/2 teaspoons	Dried tarragon leaves	2 teaspoons
2 1/2 teaspoons	Bread machine or quick active dry yeast	1 1/4 teaspoons

Make 1 1/2-Pound Recipe with bread machines that use 3 cups flour, or make 2-Pound Recipe with bread machines that use 4 cups flour.

Measure carefully, placing all ingredients in bread machine pan in the order recommended by the manufacturer.

Select Basic/White cycle. Use Medium or Light crust color. Do not use delay cycles. Remove baked bread from pan, and cool on wire rack.

▓ 1 Slice: 170 calories (35 calories from fat); 4g fat (1g saturated); 20mg cholesterol; 310mg sodium; 30g carbohydrate (1g dietary fiber); 4g protein

Smaller Can Be Just Right

Honey Sunflower Loaf (page 121)

Buttermilk Bread

If your bread machine has a 2-pound vertical pan, the loaf will be short but still will have good texture and flavor. If your bread machine has a horizontal pan, however, there isn't enough dough to make a good loaf of baked bread.

Surprised to see baking soda in a yeast bread? Baking soda works beautifully in this recipe because there are two mildly acidic ingredients—buttermilk and honey. The results give you a pleasant-tasting bread.

Here's a tasty Olive Walnut Spread to serve with this bread. Mix a 3-ounce package of softened cream cheese with 2 tablespoons milk until it is smooth and creamy. Stir in 1/2 cup finely chopped walnuts and 1/4 cup finely chopped pimiento-stuffed olives. This makes about 1 cup of spread, so cover and refrigerate any leftovers.

1-Pound Recipe (8 slices)		1 1/2-Pound Recipe (12 slices)
3/4 cup plus 2 tablespoons	Buttermilk	1 1/4 cups
2 tablespoons	Margarine or butter, softened	3 tablespoons
2 tablespoons	Honey	3 tablespoons
2 1/2 cups	Bread flour	3 1/4 cups
1 teaspoon	Salt	1 1/2 teaspoons
1/4 teaspoon	Baking soda	1/4 teaspoon
1 teaspoon	Bread machine or quick active dry yeast	1 1/2 teaspoons

Make 1-Pound Recipe with bread machines that use at least 2 cups flour, or make 1 1/2-Pound Recipe with bread machines that use at least 3 cups flour.

Measure carefully, placing all ingredients in bread machine pan in the order recommended by the manufacturer.

Select Basic/White cycle. Use Medium or Light crust color. Do not use delay cycles. Remove baked bread from pan, and cool on wire rack.

■ 1 Slice: 205 calories (30 calories from fat); 4g fat (1g saturated); 5mg cholesterol; 400mg sodium; 38g carbohydrate (1g dietary fiber); 6g protein

Honey Sunflower Loaf

1-Pound Recipe (8 slices)		1 1/2-Pound Recipe (12 slices)
2/3 cup	Water	1 cup
2 tablespoons	Vegetable oil	2 tablespoons
1 tablespoon	Honey	2 tablespoons
2 1/4 cups	Bread flour	3 1/4 cups
1/3 cup	Raw sunflower nuts	1/2 cup
1 teaspoon	Salt	1 1/2 teaspoons
1 1/4 teaspoons	Bread machine or quick active dry yeast	2 teaspoons

Make 1-Pound Recipe with bread machines that use at least 2 cups flour, or make 1 1/2-Pound Recipe with bread machines that use at least 3 cups flour.

Measure carefully, placing all ingredients in bread machine pan in the order recommended by the manufacturer.

Select Basic/White cycle. Use Medium or Light crust color. Do not use delay cycles. Remove baked bread from pan, and cool on wire rack.

■ 1 Slice: 210 calories (65 calories from fat); 7g fat (1g saturated); 0mg cholesterol; 300mg sodium; 33g carbohydrate (2g dietary fiber); 6g protein

SUCCESS TIP

If your bread machine has a 2-pound vertical pan, the loaf will be short but still will have good texture and flavor. If your bread machine has a horizontal pan, however, there isn't enough dough to make a good loaf of baked bread.

TRY THIS

If you like a bread with a slightly saltier and nuttier flavor, used toasted sunflower nuts instead of the raw nuts.

Multigrain Loaf

SUCCESS TIP

If your bread machine has a 2-pound vertical pan, the loaf will be short but still will have good texture and flavor. If your bread machine has a horizontal pan, however, there isn't enough dough to make a good loaf of baked bread.

SUCCESS TIP

You'll find 7-grain cereal in the hot-cereal section of your supermarket or at a natural foods or co-op store.

SANDWICH BOARD

Ham and cheese sandwiches are as all-American as football! Serve this triple-decker sandwich to enjoy while watching a football game, or serve it to your favorite football player after a rugged game.

1-Pound Recipe (8 slices)		1 1/2-Pound Recipe (12 slices)
3/4 cup plus 2 tablespoons	Water	1 1/4 cups
1 tablespoon	Margarine or butter, softened	2 tablespoons
1 cup	Bread flour	1 1/3 cups
3/4 cup	Whole wheat flour	1 1/3 cups
2/3 cup	7-grain or multigrain cereal	1 cup
2 tablespoons	Packed brown sugar	3 tablespoons
1 teaspoon	Salt	1 1/4 teaspoons
2 teaspoons	Bread machine or quick active dry yeast	2 1/2 teaspoons

Make 1-Pound Recipe with bread machines that use 2 cups flour, or make 1 1/2-Pound Recipe with bread machines that use 3 cups flour.

Measure carefully, placing all ingredients in bread machine pan in the order recommended by the manufacturer.

Select Whole Wheat or Basic/White cycle. Use Medium or Light crust color. Remove baked bread from pan, and cool on wire rack.

■ 1 Slice: 135 calories (20 calories from fat); 2g fat (0g saturated); 0mg cholesterol; 330mg sodium; 27g carbohydrate (2g dietary fiber); 4g protein

Multigrain Loaf

Caraway Rye Bread

SUCCESS TIP

If your bread machine has a 2-pound vertical pan, the loaf will be short but still will have good texture and flavor. If your bread machine has a horizontal pan, however, there isn't enough dough to make a good loaf of baked bread.

SANDWICH BOARD

To make this bread "picture perfect," try this delicious tangy cheese spread. Mix a 3-ounce package of softened cream cheese with 2 tablespoons milk until smooth and creamy. Stir in 1/2 cup finely shredded aged Swiss cheese and 1 tablespoon of chopped fresh chives or green onion. This makes about 2/3 cup Swiss Cheese and Chives spread, so cover and refrigerate leftovers—if there are any!

1-Pound Recipe (8 slices)		1 1/2-Pound Recipe (12 slices)
3/4 cup	Water	1 cup plus 3 tablespoons
2 teaspoons	Margarine or butter, softened	1 tablespoon
1 1/2 cups	Bread flour	2 1/2 cups
1/2 cup	Rye flour	3/4 cup
1 tablespoon	Dry milk	2 tablespoons
1 tablespoon	Sugar	2 tablespoons
1 teaspoon	Salt	1 1/2 teaspoons
1/8 teaspoon	Caraway seed	3/4 teaspoon
1 1/4 teaspoons	Bread machine or quick active dry yeast	2 1/4 teaspoons

Make 1-Pound Recipe with bread machines that use 2 cups flour, or make 1 1/2-Pound Recipe with bread machines that use 3 cups flour.

Measure carefully, placing all ingredients in bread machine pan in the order recommended by the manufacturer.

Select Basic/White cycle. Use Medium or Light crust color. Remove baked bread from pan, and cool on wire rack.

■ 1 Slice: 125 calories (10 calories from fat); 1g fat (0g saturated); 0mg cholesterol; 310mg sodium; 27g carbohydrate (2g dietary fiber); 4g protein

Caraway Rye Bread

Peanut Butter Bread

1-Pound Recipe (8 slices)		1 1/2-Pound Recipe (12 slices)
2/3 cup	Water	1 cup plus 1 tablespoon
1/4 cup	Peanut butter	1/2 cup
2 cups	Bread flour	3 cups
2 tablespoons	Packed brown sugar	3 tablespoons
3/4 teaspoon	Salt	1 teaspoon
1 1/4 teaspoons	Bread machine or quick active dry yeast	2 teaspoons

Make 1-Pound Recipe with bread machines that use 2 cups flour, or make 1 1/2-Pound Recipe with bread machines that use 3 cups flour.

Measure carefully, placing all ingredients in bread machine pan in the order recommended by the manufacturer.

Select Sweet or Basic/White cycle. Use Medium or Light crust color. Remove baked bread from pan, and cool on wire rack.

■ 1 Slice: 175 calories (35 calories from fat); 4g fat (1g saturated); 0mg cholesterol; 260mg sodium; 31g carbohydrate (2g dietary fiber); 6g protein

Potato Chive Bread

1-Pound Recipe (8 slices)		1 1/2-Pound Recipe (12 slices)
3/4 cup	Water	1 cup plus 2 tablespoons
1 tablespoon	Margarine or butter, softened	2 tablespoons
2 cups	Bread flour	3 cups
1/3 cup	Mashed potato mix (dry)	1/2 cup
2 tablespoons	Chopped fresh chives	1/4 cup
2 teaspoons	Sugar	1 tablespoon
1 teaspoon	Salt	1 1/2 teaspoons
1 3/4 teaspoons	Bread machine or quick active dry yeast	2 3/4 teaspoons

Make 1-Pound Recipe with bread machines that use 2 cups flour, or make 1 1/2–Pound Recipe with bread machines that use 3 cups flour.

Measure carefully, placing all ingredients in bread machine pan in the order recommended by the manufacturer.

Select Basic/White cycle. Use Medium or Light crust color. Do not use delay cycles. Remove baked bread from pan, and cool on wire rack.

■ 1 Slice: 145 calories (20 calories from fat); 2g fat (0g saturated); 0mg cholesterol; 290mg sodium; 29g carbohydrate (1g dietary fiber); 4g protein

SUCCESS TIP

If your bread machine has a 2-pound vertical pan, the loaf will be short but still will have good texture and flavor. If your bread machine has a horizontal pan, however, there isn't enough dough to make a good loaf of baked bread.

TRY THIS

Instead of fresh chives, use 1 tablespoon freeze-dried chives in the 1-pound loaf or 2 tablespoons in the 1 1/2-pound loaf. For a flavor twist, try 3/4 teaspoon dried tarragon leaves in the 1-pound loaf and 1 teaspoon in the 1 1/2-pound loaf.

Garlic Basil Bread

SUCCESS TIP

If your bread machine has a 2-pound vertical pan, the loaf will be short but still will have good texture and flavor. If your bread machine has a horizontal pan, however, there isn't enough dough to make a good loaf of baked bread.

SANDWICH BOARD

Here's how to make quick and easy Parmesan Cheese Breadsticks. Spread toasted slices of this garlicky basil bread with margarine or butter. Sprinkle generously with grated or finely shredded Parmesan cheese. Cut each piece of toast into 1-inch sticks. Kids love them, especially for dunking into a bowl of their favorite soup for a quick lunch.

1-Pound Recipe (8 slices)		1 1/2-Pound Recipe (12 slices)
3/4 cup	Water	1 cup plus 1 tablespoon
2 teaspoons	Margarine or butter, softened	1 tablespoon
1 clove	Garlic, finely chopped	2 cloves
2 cups	Bread flour	3 cups
1 tablespoon	Dry milk	2 tablespoons
1 tablespoon	Sugar	2 tablespoons
1 teaspoon	Salt	1 1/2 teaspoons
1 teaspoon	Dried basil leaves	1 1/2 teaspoons
1 1/2 teaspoons	Bread machine or quick active dry yeast	2 1/4 teaspoons

Make 1-Pound Recipe with bread machines that use 2 cups flour, or make 1 1/2-Pound Recipe with bread machines that use 3 cups flour.

Measure carefully, placing all ingredients in bread machine pan in the order recommended by the manufacturer.

Select Basic/White cycle. Use Medium or Light crust color. Do not use delay cycles. Remove baked bread from pan, and cool on wire rack.

■ 1 Slice: 140 calories (20 calories from fat); 2g fat (0g saturated); 0mg cholesterol; 310mg sodium; 28g carbohydrate (1Xg dietary fiber); 4g protein

Cheddar Cheese and Olive Bread

1-Pound Recipe (8 slices)		1 1/2-Pound Recipe (12 slices)
3/4 cup	Water	1 cup plus 2 tablespoons
2 cups	Bread flour	3 cups
3/4 cup	Shredded sharp Cheddar cheese	1 1/4 cups
1 tablespoon	Sugar	1 tablespoon plus 1 1/2 teaspoons
1/2 teaspoon	Salt	3/4 teaspoon
3/4 teaspoon	Bread machine or quick active dry yeast	1 1/4 teaspoons
1/2 cup	Small pimiento-stuffed olives, well drained	3/4 cup

Make 1-Pound Recipe with bread machines that use 2 cups flour, or make 1 1/2-Pound Recipe with bread machines that use 3 cups flour.

Measure carefully, placing all ingredients except olives in bread machine pan in the order recommended by the manufacturer. Add olives at the Raisin/Nut signal.

Select Basic/White cycle. Use Medium or Light crust color. Do not use delay cycles. Remove baked bread from pan, and cool on wire rack.

■ 1 Slice: 175 calories (45 calories from fat); 5g fat (2g saturated); 10mg cholesterol; 430mg sodium; 28g carbohydrate (1g dietary fiber); 6g protein

SUCCESS TIP

If your bread machine has a 2-pound vertical pan, the loaf will be short but still will have good texture and flavor. If your bread machine has a horizontal pan, however, there isn't enough dough to make a good loaf of baked bread.

SUCCESS TIP

If your bread machine doesn't have a Raisin/Nut signal, add the olives 5 to 10 minutes before the last kneading cycle ends. Check your bread machine's use-and-care book to find out how long the last cycle runs.

DID YOU KNOW?

Cheddar cheese originated in Cheddar, a village in the Somerset region of England. It can range from mild to sharp in flavor and from white to bright orange in color. We liked the stronger flavor of the sharp Cheddar in this bread, but you can use a mild Cheddar cheese instead. A white Cheddar will give you the same great flavor, but the bread will not have the yellowish-orange color.

Double-Corn Jalapeño Bread

SUCCESS TIP

If your bread machine has a 2-pound vertical pan, the loaf will be short but still will have good texture and flavor. If your bread machine has a horizontal pan, however, there isn't enough dough to make a good loaf of baked bread. We also found that we didn't have good results in bread machines with glass-dome lids.

DID YOU KNOW?

Jalapeño chilies are named after Jalapa, the capital of Veracruz, Mexico. The seeds and membrane inside the chili contain a compound called capsaicin, which creates the heat of the chili. This compound also can burn your skin and eyes, so be sure to wear plastic gloves when handling chilies and wash your hands thoroughly when finished.

SANDWICH BOARD

This Chili Cheddar Spread is a great way to use any extra corn. Mix a 3-ounce package of softened cream cheese with 2 tablespoons milk until smooth and creamy. Stir in 1/3 cup shredded Cheddar cheese, 1/4 cup whole kernel corn, 3/4 teaspoon chili powder and a sliced green onion. This makes about 3/4 cup spread, so cover and refrigerate any leftovers.

1-Pound Recipe (8 slices)		1 1/2-Pound Recipe (12 slices)
1/2 cup	Water	3/4 cup plus 2 tablespoons
1/2 cup	Frozen whole kernel corn, thawed	2/3 cup
1 tablespoon	Margarine or butter, softened	2 tablespoons
2 teaspoons	Chopped jalapeño chili	1 tablespoon
2 cups	Bread flour	3 1/4 cups
1/4 cup	Cornmeal	1/3 cup
1 tablespoon	Sugar	2 tablespoons
1 teaspoon	Salt	1 1/2 teaspoons
1 1/2 teaspoons	Bread machine or quick active dry yeast	2 1/2 teaspoons

Make 1-Pound Recipe with bread machines that use 2 cups flour, or make 1 1/2-Pound Recipe with bread machines that use at least 3 cups flour.

Measure carefully, placing all ingredients in bread machine pan in the order recommended by the manufacturer.

Select Basic/White cycle. Use Medium or Light crust color. Do not use delay cycles. Remove baked bread from pan, and cool on wire rack.

■ 1 Slice: 160 calories (20 calories from fat); 2g fat (0g saturated); 0mg cholesterol; 320mg sodium; 33g carbohydrate (2g dietary fiber); 4g protein

Double-Corn Jalapeño Bread

Spicy Apple Bread

SUCCESS TIP

If your bread machine has a 2-pound vertical pan, the loaf will be short but still will have good texture and flavor. If your bread machine has a horizontal pan, however, there isn't enough dough to make a good loaf of baked bread.

TRY THIS

If you are out of apple pie spice, you can make your own mixture. For 1 1/2 teaspoons, use 3/4 teaspoon ground cinnamon, 1/4 teaspoon ground ginger, 1/4 teaspoon ground allspice and 1/4 teaspoon ground nutmeg. For 2 1/2 teaspoons, use 1 1/2 teaspoons ground cinnamon, 1/2 teaspoon ground ginger, 1/4 teaspoon ground allspice and 1/4 teaspoon ground nutmeg.

SANDWICH BOARD

Start the day off with a slice of warm toasted spicy apple bread generously spread with Honey Peanut Butter Spread. Mix a 3-ounce package of softened cream cheese with 2 tablespoons milk until smooth and creamy. Stir in 1/4 cup crunchy peanut butter and 1 tablespoon of honey. This makes about 2/3 cup of spread, so cover and refrigerate any leftovers. It will be ready when you want another peanutty treat!

1-Pound Recipe (8 slices)		1 1/2-Pound Recipe (12 slices)
2/3 cup	Water	1 cup plus 1 tablespoon
1 tablespoon	Margarine or butter, softened	2 tablespoons
2 cups	Bread flour	3 cups
1/4 cup	Cut-up dried apples	1/3 cup
1 tablespoon	Dry milk	2 tablespoons
1 tablespoon	Sugar	2 tablespoons
1 teaspoon	Salt	1 1/2 teaspoons
1 1/2 teaspoons	Apple pie spice	2 1/2 teaspoons
1 1/2 teaspoons	Bread machine or quick active dry yeast	2 teaspoons

Make 1-Pound Recipe with bread machines that use 2 cups flour, or make 1 1/2-Pound Recipe with bread machines that use 3 cups flour.

Measure carefully, placing all ingredients in bread machine pan in the order recommended by the manufacturer.

Select Sweet or Basic/White cycle. Use Medium or Light crust color. Remove baked bread from pan, and cool on wire rack.

■ 1 Slice: 150 calories (20 calories from fat); 2g fat (0g saturated); 0mg cholesterol; 320mg sodium; 30g carbohydrate (1g dietary fiber); 4g protein

Choco-Banana Bread (page 139) and Spicy Apple Bread

Almond Chocolate Chip Bread

SUCCESS TIP

If your bread machine has a 2-pound vertical pan, the loaf will be short but still will have good texture and flavor. If your bread machine has a horizontal pan, however, there isn't enough dough to make a good loaf of baked bread.

SUCCESS TIP

If your bread machine doesn't have a Raisin/Nut signal, add the almonds 5 to 10 minutes before the last kneading cycle ends. Check your bread machine's use-and-care book to find out how long the last cycle runs.

TRY THIS

Toast the almonds to give this chocolate bread even more almond boost. Sprinkle the almonds in a heavy skillet. Cook over medium-low heat, stirring them frequently, until they are golden brown and you can smell the toasty almond aroma. Pour them out of the skillet so they don't continue to brown, and let them cool before using.

1-Pound Recipe (8 slices)		1 1/2-Pound Recipe (12 slices)
3/4 cup plus 1 tablespoon	Water	1 cup plus 2 tablespoons
1 tablespoon	Margarine or butter, softened	2 tablespoons
1/4 teaspoon	Vanilla	1/2 teaspoon
2 cups	Bread flour	3 cups
1/2 cup	Semisweet chocolate chips	3/4 cup
2 tablespoons	Sugar	3 tablespoons
2 teaspoons	Dry milk	1 tablespoon
1/2 teaspoon	Salt	3/4 teaspoon
1 teaspoon	Bread machine or quick active dry yeast	1 1/2 teaspoons
1/4 cup	Sliced almonds	1/3 cup

Make 1-Pound Recipe with bread machines that use 2 cups flour, or make 1 1/2-Pound Recipe with bread machines that use 3 cups flour.

Measure carefully, placing all ingredients except almonds in bread machine pan in the order recommended by the manufacturer. Add almonds at the Raisin/Nut signal.

Select Sweet or Basic/White cycle. Use Medium or Light crust color. Remove baked bread from pan, and cool on wire rack.

■ 1 Slice: 225 calories (65 calories from fat); 7g fat (2g saturated); 0mg cholesterol; 320mg sodium; 37g carbohydrate (2g dietary fiber); 5g protein

Almond Chocolate Chip Bread

Cranberry Whole Wheat Bread

SUCCESS TIP

If your bread machine has a 2-pound vertical pan, the loaf will be short but still will have good texture and flavor. If your bread machine has a horizontal pan, however, there isn't enough dough to make a good loaf of baked bread.

SUCCESS TIP

If your bread machine doesn't have a Raisin/Nut signal, add the cranberries 5 to 10 minutes before the last kneading cycle ends. Check your bread machine's use-and-care book to find out how long the last cycle runs.

TRY THIS

You can use raisins if you don't have dried cranberries handy. Actually, any dried berry will do—you also may want to try dried cherries or blueberries. For a triple-berry treat, mix cranberries, cherries and blueberries together, and use the same amount as if you were using just the cranberries.

SANDWICH BOARD

Spread slices of this cranberry-studded bread with cranberry relish. Stack on slices of cold turkey and Swiss cheese, and top with your favorite kind of lettuce or sprouts and gobble it up!

1-Pound Recipe (8 slices)		1 1/2-Pound Recipe (12 slices)
3/4 cup	Water	1 cup plus 2 tablespoons
2 tablespoons	Honey	1/4 cup
1 tablespoon	Margarine or butter, softened	2 tablespoons
1 1/4 cups	Bread flour	2 cups
3/4 cup	Whole wheat flour	1 1/4 cups
1 teaspoon	Salt	1 1/2 teaspoons
1/4 teaspoon	Ground mace	3/4 teaspoon
1 1/4 teaspoons	Bread machine or quick active dry yeast	2 teaspoons
1/3 cup	Dried cranberries	1/2 cup

Make 1-Pound Recipe with bread machines that use 2 cups flour, or make 1 1/2-Pound Recipe with bread machines that use 3 cups flour.

Measure carefully, placing all ingredients except cranberries in bread machine pan in the order recommended by the manufacturer. Add cranberries at the Raisin/Nut signal.

Select Whole Wheat or Basic/White cycle. Use Medium or Light crust color. Do not use delay cycles. Remove baked bread from pan, and cool on wire rack.

■ 1 Slice: 155 calories (10 calories from fat); 1g fat (0g saturated); 0mg cholesterol; 300mg sodium; 34g carbohydrate (4g dietary fiber); 4g protein

Cranberry Whole Wheat Bread

Greek Olive Bread

SUCCESS TIP

If your bread machine has a 2-pound vertical pan, the loaf will be short but still will have good texture and flavor. If your bread machine has a horizontal pan, however, there isn't enough dough to make a good loaf of baked bread.

SUCCESS TIP

If your bread machine doesn't have a Raisin/Nut signal, add the olives 5 to 10 minutes before the last kneading cycle ends. Check your bread machine's use-and-care book to find out how long the last cycle runs.

DID YOU KNOW?

Kalamata is a popular imported ripe olive from Greece. This purple-black olive is available packed in olive oil or vinegar; either type will work in this bread recipe. Not all Kalamata olives are available pitted, so check with your grocer for the pitted ones.

1-Pound Recipe (8 slices)		1 1/2-Pound Recipe (12 slices)
3/4 cup plus 1 tablespoon	Water	1 cup plus 2 tablespoons
2 teaspoons	Olive or vegetable oil	1 tablespoon
2 cups	Bread flour	3 cups
1 tablespoon	Sugar	2 tablespoons
1/2 teaspoon	Salt	1 teaspoon
3/4 teaspoon	Bread machine or quick active dry yeast	1 1/4 teaspoons
1/3 cup	Kalamata or Greek olives, pitted and coarsely chopped	1/2 cup

Make 1–Pound Recipe with bread machines that use 2 cups flour, or make 1 1/2-Pound Recipe with bread machines that use 3 cups flour.

Measure carefully, placing all ingredients except olives in bread machine pan in the order recommended by the manufacturer. Add olives at the Raisin/Nut signal.

Select Basic/White cycle. Use Medium or Light crust color. Do not use delay cycles. Remove baked bread from pan, and cool on wire rack.

■ 1 Slice: 140 calories (20 calories from fat); 2g fat (0g saturated); 0mg cholesterol; 200mg sodium; 28g carbohydrate (1g dietary fiber); 4g protein

Choco-Banana Bread

1-Pound Recipe (8 slices)		1 1/2-Pound Recipe (12 slices)
1/2 cup	Water	2/3 cup
1/3 cup	Mashed ripe bananas	2/3 cup
1 tablespoon	Margarine or butter, softened	2 tablespoons
1 egg white	Egg	1 whole egg
2 cups	Bread flour	3 cups
2 tablespoons	Sugar	3 tablespoons
3/4 teaspoon	Salt	1 1/4 teaspoons
1 1/2 teaspoons	Bread machine or quick active dry yeast	2 1/4 teaspoons
1/3 cup	Miniature semisweet chocolate chips	1/2 cup

Make 1-Pound Recipe with bread machines that use 2 cups flour, or make 1 1/2-Pound Recipe with bread machines that use 3 cups flour.

Measure carefully, placing all ingredients except chocolate chips in bread machine pan in the order recommended by the manufacturer. Add chocolate chips at the Raisin/Nut signal.

Select Sweet or Basic/White cycle. Use Medium or Light crust color. Do not use delay cycles. Remove baked bread from pan, and cool on wire rack.

■ 1 Slice: 190 calories (35 calories from fat); 4g fat (0g saturated); 0mg cholesterol; 250mg sodium; 36g carbohydrate (2g dietary fiber); 5g protein

SUCCESS TIP

If your bread machine has a 2-pound vertical pan, the loaf will be short but still will have good texture and flavor. If your bread machine has a horizontal pan, however, there isn't enough dough to make a good loaf of baked bread.

SUCCESS TIP

Depending on the ripeness of your bananas, the dough may need a little more flour than the recipe recommends. Five minutes after the cycle begins, check the consistency of the dough. If the dough is not forming a ball and seems too wet, add more flour, 1 tablespoon at a time, until a soft dough forms.

SUCCESS TIP

If your bread machine doesn't have a Raisin/Nut signal, add the chocolate chips 5 to 10 minutes before the last kneading cycle ends. Check your bread machine's use-and-care book to find out how long the last cycle runs.

Rustic Loaves and Flatbreads

Chicken Fajita Pizza (page 172)

Old-World Rye Bread

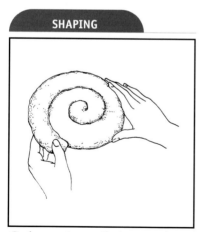

Curl rope into coil shape; tuck end under.

1 loaf, 16 slices

2/3 cup water

2 tablespoons vegetable oil

2/3 cup buttermilk

2 1/4 cups bread flour

1 cup rye flour

1/3 cup mashed potato mix (dry)

2 tablespoons packed brown sugar

1 1/4 teaspoons salt

1 teaspoon caraway seed

2 teaspoons bread machine or quick active dry yeast

Cornmeal

Additional caraway seed, if desired

Measure carefully, placing all ingredients except cornmeal and additional caraway seed in bread machine pan in the order recommended by the manufacturer.

Select Dough/Manual cycle. Do not use delay cycles.

Remove dough from pan, using lightly floured hands. Cover and let rest 10 minutes on lightly floured surface.

Grease large cookie sheet; sprinkle with cornmeal. Roll dough into 25-inch rope. Curl rope into coil shape; tuck end under. Place on cookie sheet. Cover and let rise in warm place 30 to 45 minutes or until double. (Dough is ready if indentation remains when touched.)

Heat oven to 400°. Brush water over loaf; sprinkle with cornmeal and additional caraway seed. Bake 23 to 28 minutes or until loaf is golden brown and sounds hollow when tapped. Remove from cookie sheet to wire rack; cool.

■ 1 Slice: 125 calories (30 calories from fat); 3g fat (1g saturated); 2mg cholesterol; 160mg sodium; 23g carbohydrate (2g dietary fiber); 3g protein

Triple-Seed Wheat Bread

TRY THIS

Be creative and use other seeds to top this bread. Try a teaspoon of dill or celery seed for the poppy seed, or anise, cardamom or caraway seed for the fennel seed.

SHAPING

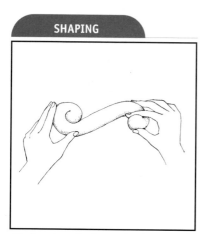

Curl each end of rope in the opposite direction to form an "S" shape.

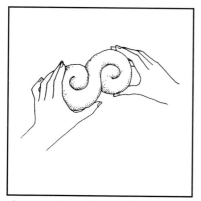

Continue the coiling until ends meet. The bread won't lose the "S" shape during rising and baking if it is formed tight enough.

1 loaf, 16 slices

1 cup plus 1 tablespoon water

2 tablespoons margarine or butter, softened

1 1/2 cups bread flour

1 1/2 cups whole wheat flour

2 tablespoons sugar

1 1/2 teaspoons salt

1 1/2 teaspoons poppy seed

1 1/2 teaspoons sesame seed

1 teaspoon fennel seed

2 teaspoons bread machine or quick active dry yeast

1 egg white, beaten

1 teaspoon poppy seed

1 teaspoon sesame seed

1 teaspoon fennel seed

Measure carefully, placing all ingredients except egg white and 1 teaspoon each poppy seed, sesame seed and fennel seed in bread machine pan in the order recommended by the manufacturer.

Select Dough/Manual cycle. Do not use delay cycles.

Remove dough from pan, using lightly floured hands. Cover and let rest 10 minutes on lightly floured surface.

Grease large cookie sheet. Roll dough into 20-inch rope. Place on cookie sheet. Curl each end of rope in the opposite direction to form a coiled "S" shape. Cover and let rise in warm place 30 to 40 minutes or until almost double.

Heat oven to 375°. Brush egg white over loaf; sprinkle with 1 teaspoon each poppy seed, sesame seed and fennel seed. Bake 20 to 25 minutes or until loaf is golden brown and sounds hollow when tapped. Remove from cookie sheet to wire rack; cool.

■ 1 Slice: 100 calories (20 calories from fat); 2g fat (0g saturated); 0mg cholesterol; 240mg sodium; 19g carbohydrate (2g dietary fiber); 3g protein

Triple-Seed Wheat Bread

Sage Raisin Wheat Bread

SUCCESS TIP

If your bread machine doesn't have a Raisin/Nut signal, add the raisins 5 to 10 minutes before the last kneading cycle ends. Check your bread machine's use-and-care book for how long the last cycle runs.

SHAPING

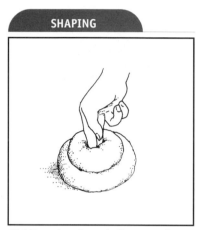

Holding thumb and first two fingers together, push into center of dough until almost touching the cookie sheet.

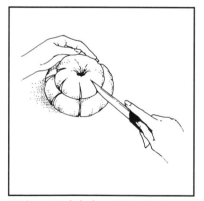

Make vertical slashes, 1/4-inch deep, on sides of each ball about 2 inches apart. Be sure to push the smaller ball of dough deeply into the large ball, or it will pop out during rising or baking.

1 loaf, 16 slices

1 1/4 cups water

2 tablespoons margarine or butter, softened

1 1/2 cups bread flour

1 1/2 cups whole wheat flour

2 tablespoons sugar

1 1/2 teaspoons salt

3/4 teaspoon crumbled dried sage leaves

1 3/4 teaspoons bread machine or quick active dry yeast

3/4 cup golden raisins

1 egg, beaten

Measure carefully, placing all ingredients except raisins and egg in bread machine pan in the order recommended by the manufacturer. Add raisins at the Raisin/Nut signal.

Select Dough/Manual cycle. Do not use delay cycles.

Remove dough from pan, using lightly floured hands. Cover and let rest 10 minutes on lightly floured surface.

Grease large cookie sheet. Cut off one-third of the dough; shape into small ball (about 3 inches). Shape remaining dough into large ball (about 5 inches). Place large ball on cookie sheet; place small ball on large ball. Holding thumb and first two fingers together, push into the middle of the small ball, pushing through center of dough until almost touching cookie sheet. Cover and let rise in warm place 30 to 45 minutes or until double. (Dough is ready if indentation remains when touched.)

Heat oven to 400°. Brush egg over loaf. Make vertical slashes, 1/4 inch deep, on sides of each ball about 2 inches apart, using sharp knife. Bake 18 to 20 minutes or until loaf is deep golden brown and sounds hollow when tapped. Remove from cookie sheet to wire rack; cool.

■ 1 Slice: 120 calories (20 calories from fat); 2g fat (0g saturated); 5mg cholesterol; 240mg sodium; 25g carbohydrate (2g dietary fiber); 3g protein

Sage Raisin Wheat Bread

Chocolate Coffee Bread

SUCCESS TIP

If your bread machine doesn't have a Raisin/Nut signal, add the chips 5 to 10 minutes before the last kneading cycle ends. Check your bread machine's use-and-care book for how long the last cycle runs.

SHAPING

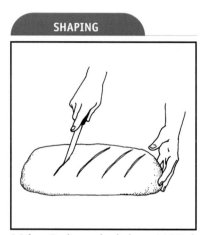

Make 5 diagonal slashes, 1/4-inch deep, across top of loaf.

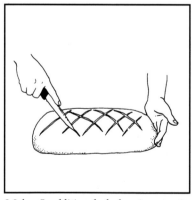

Make 5 additional slashes in opposite direction to make ×-shaped cuts.

1 loaf, 16 slices

1 cup water

2 tablespoons margarine or butter, softened

3 cups bread flour

1/3 cup packed brown sugar

1 tablespoon instant coffee granules

1 teaspoon salt

2 1/4 teaspoons bread machine or quick active dry yeast

1/2 cup semisweet chocolate chips

1 egg, beaten

1 teaspoon instant coffee granules

1 tablespoon granulated sugar

Measure carefully, placing all ingredients except chocolate chips, egg, 1 teaspoon instant coffee granules and the granulated sugar in bread machine pan in the order recommended by the manufacturer. Add chocolate chips at the Raisin/Nut signal.

Select Dough/Manual cycle. Do not use delay cycles.

Remove dough from pan, using lightly floured hands. Cover and let rest 10 minutes on lightly floured surface.

Grease large cookie sheet. Shape dough into 10 × 3-inch rectangle on cookie sheet. Cover and let rise in warm place 40 to 50 minutes or until double. (Dough is ready if indentation remains when touched.)

Heat oven to 400°. Make 5 diagonal slashes, 1/4 inch deep, across top of loaf, using sharp knife. Make 5 additional slashes in opposite direction to make ×-shaped cuts. Brush egg over top of loaf. Mix 1 teaspoon coffee granules and the granulated sugar; sprinkle over loaf. Bake 18 to 20 minutes or until loaf is golden brown and sounds hollow when tapped. Remove from cookie sheet to wire rack; cool.

■ 1 Slice: 140 calories (30 calories from fat); 3g fat (1g saturated); 0mg cholesterol; 170mg sodium; 26g carbohydrate (1g dietary fiber); 3g protein

DO-AHEAD NOTE: Cover the shaped dough on the cookie sheet with plastic wrap. Refrigerate from 4 hours up to 24 hours. Before baking, remove plastic wrap, cover with kitchen towel and let rise in a warm place about 2 hours or until double. Then top and bake.

Chocolate Coffee Bread

Buttermilk Granola Bread

SUCCESS TIP

If your bread machine doesn't have a Raisin/Nut signal, add the granola 5 to 10 minutes before the last kneading cycle ends. Check your bread machine's use-and-care book for how long the last cycle runs.

DO-AHEAD NOTE

Cover the round loaf on the cookie sheet with plastic wrap. Refrigerate it from 4 hours up to 48 hours. Before baking, remove plastic wrap, cover with kitchen towel and let rise in a warm place about 2 hours or until it is about 7 1/2 inches in diameter. Then cut the top and bake the loaf as the recipe tells you.

SHAPING

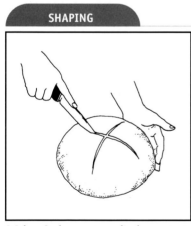

Make 2 long perpendicular cuts to resemble a large plus sign on top of loaf.

1 loaf, 16 slices

1/2 cup water

1/2 cup buttermilk

2 tablespoons honey

2 tablespoons margarine or butter, softened

3 cups bread flour

1 1/2 teaspoons salt

1 1/2 teaspoons bread machine or quick active dry yeast

2/3 cup granola (any flavor)

Measure carefully, placing all ingredients except granola in bread machine pan in the order recommended by the manufacturer. Add granola at the Raisin/Nut signal.

Select Dough/Manual cycle. Do not use delay cycles.

Remove dough from pan, using lightly floured hands. Cover and let rest 10 minutes on lightly floured surface.

Grease large cookie sheet. Shape dough into round loaf, about 5 inches in diameter and 3 inches high. Place on cookie sheet. Cover and let rise in warm place 45 to 60 minutes or until about 7 1/2 inches in diameter.

Heat oven to 400°. Make 2 long perpendicular cuts in top of loaf to resemble a large plus sign (+), using sharp knife. Brush or spray top of loaf with water. Bake 20 to 25 minutes or until loaf is golden brown and sounds hollow when tapped. Remove from cookie sheet to wire rack; cool.

■ 1 Slice: 120 calories (20 calories from fat); 2g fat (1g saturated); 1mg cholesterol; 250mg sodium; 23g carbohydrate (1g dietary fiber); 3g protein

Cottage Dill Loaf

SUCCESS TIP

Spraying the loaf with water before and during the first 10 minutes of baking will give you a crustier loaf, and the inside of the bread will be soft and chewy. Use a spray bottle that has a fine mist, so the water is evenly distributed over the loaf.

SUCCESS TIP

The dough may look too dry at the beginning of mixing. Don't add additional liquid, however, until the dough has mixed for a few minutes because as the cottage cheese breaks up, it will add moisture to the dough.

SHAPING

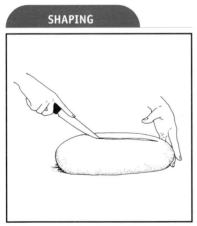

Make long slash, 1/4-inch deep, down center of loaf.

1 loaf, 16 slices

1 cup water

1 tablespoon margarine or butter, softened

1/2 cup small curd creamed cottage cheese

3 1/2 cups bread flour

1 tablespoon sugar

1 tablespoon dill seed

1 tablespoon instant minced onion

1 teaspoon salt

1 1/2 teaspoons bread machine or quick active dry yeast

1 teaspoon instant minced onion

1 teaspoon dill seed

Measure carefully, placing all ingredients except 1 teaspoon onion and 1 teaspoon dill seed in bread machine pan in the order recommended by the manufacturer.

Select Dough/Manual cycle. Do not use delay cycles.

Remove dough from pan, using lightly floured hands. Cover and let rest 10 minutes on lightly floured surface.

Grease large cookie sheet. Shape dough into oval, 12 × 4 inches, tapering both ends slightly. Place on cookie sheet. Cover and let rise in warm place 30 to 45 minutes or until double. (Dough is ready if indentation remains when touched.)

Heat oven to 375°. Spray water over loaf; sprinkle with 1 teaspoon onion and 1 teaspoon dill seed. Make long slash, 1/4 inch deep, down center of loaf, using sharp knife. Bake 10 minutes, spraying 3 times with water. Bake 15 to 20 minutes longer or until loaf is golden brown and sounds hollow when tapped. Remove from cookie sheet to wire rack; cool.

■ 1 Slice: 105 calories (20 calories from fat); 2g fat (0g saturated); 1mg cholesterol; 190mg sodium; 19g carbohydrate (1g dietary fiber); 4g protein

Rosemary Apricot Bread

SUCCESS TIP

If your bread machine doesn't have a Raisin/Nut signal, add the apricots 5 to 10 minutes before the last kneading cycle ends. Check your bread machine's use-and-care book to find out how long the last cycle runs.

TRY THIS

The wonderful lemony, pine flavor of rosemary also complements other dried fruits. For a flavor twist, dried peaches or apples, cut into 1/2-inch pieces, can be used instead of the apricots.

SHAPING

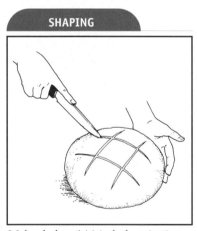

Make slashes, 1/4-inch deep, in tic-tac-toe pattern on top of loaf.

1 loaf, 16 slices

1 cup plus 1 tablespoon water

1 tablespoon margarine or butter, softened

3 cups bread flour

1 tablespoon sugar

1 1/2 teaspoons salt

1 teaspoon dried rosemary leaves

2 1/4 teaspoons bread machine or quick active dry yeast

2/3 cup dried apricots, cut into fourths

Cornmeal

Measure carefully, placing all ingredients except apricots and cornmeal in bread machine pan in the order recommended by the manufacturer. Add apricots at the Raisin/Nut signal.

Select Dough/Manual cycle. Do not use delay cycles.

Remove dough from pan, using lightly floured hands. Cover and let rest 10 minutes on lightly floured surface.

Grease large cookie sheet; sprinkle with cornmeal. Shape dough into round loaf, about 5 inches in diameter and 3 inches high. Roll top of loaf on lightly floured surface; place floured side up on cookie sheet. Cover and let rise in warm place 40 to 50 minutes or until about 7 1/2 inches in diameter.

Heat oven to 400°. Make slashes, 1/4 inch deep, in tic-tac-toe pattern on top of loaf, using sharp knife. Spray with water. Bake 10 minutes, spraying 3 times with water. Bake 20 to 25 minutes longer or until loaf is golden brown and sounds hollow when tapped. Remove from cookie sheet to wire rack; cool.

■ 1 Slice: 90 calories (10 calories from fat); 1g fat (0g saturated); 0mg cholesterol; 230mg sodium; 20g carbohydrate (1g dietary fiber); 2g protein

Lemon Anise Bread

SHAPING

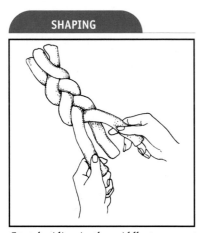

Start braiding in the middle to prevent the dough from stretching and making the shape uneven. Also, keep the braid slightly loose, so there is room for the dough to rise.

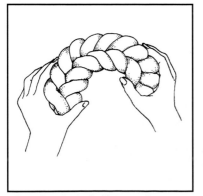

Shape braid into half-moon shape.

1 loaf, 16 slices

1 cup plus 1 tablespoon water

2 tablespoons margarine or butter, softened

3 cups bread flour

1/3 cup sugar

1 teaspoon salt

1 1/2 teaspoons anise seed, crushed

1 1/2 teaspoons grated lemon peel

2 1/2 teaspoons bread machine or quick active dry yeast

1 egg, beaten

Measure carefully, placing all ingredients except egg in bread machine pan in the order recommended by the manufacturer.

Select Dough/Manual cycle. Do not use delay cycles.

Remove dough from pan, using lightly floured hands. Cover and let rest 10 minutes on lightly floured surface.

Grease large cookie sheet. Divide dough into thirds. Roll each third into 20-inch rope. Braid ropes gently and loosely, starting at the middle. Pinch ends together; tuck the ends under the braid. Place on cookie sheet. Shape braid into large half-moon shape. Cover and let rise in warm place 45 to 60 minutes or until double. (Dough is ready if indentation remains when touched.)

Heat oven to 400°. Brush egg over loaf. Bake 20 to 25 minutes or until loaf is golden brown and sounds hollow when tapped. Serve warm, or cool on wire rack.

■ 1 Slice: 115 calories (20 calories from fat); 2g fat (0g saturated); 0mg cholesterol; 170mg sodium; 22g carbohydrate (1g dietary fiber); 3g protein

Roasted Pepper Focaccia (page 167) and Lemon Anise Bread

Sourdough Loaf

SUCCESS TIP

If you would like a more decorative loaf, slash the top of the loaf before baking. Check out pages 150 and 154 for some ideas.

DID YOU KNOW?

San Francisco is known for its superior sourdough bread. However, bread made in San Francisco will taste different than bread made in your town. Why is that? It can be due to the air and water, which vary from area to area. There are natural airborne molds that affect the starter. Also water can affect how the starter works and the general flavor of the bread.

1 loaf, 16 slices

1 1/4 cups Sourdough Starter (page 26)

1/4 cup water

3 cups bread flour

1 tablespoon sugar

1 teaspoon salt

1 teaspoon bread machine or quick active dry yeast

Cornmeal

Measure carefully, placing all ingredients except cornmeal in bread machine pan in the order recommended by the manufacturer.

Select Dough/Manual cycle. Do not use delay cycles.

Remove dough from pan, using lightly floured hands. Cover and let rest 10 minutes on lightly floured surface.

Grease large cookie sheet; sprinkle with cornmeal. Shape dough into round loaf, about 6 inches in diameter, on cookie sheet. Cover and let rise in warm place 35 to 40 minutes or until almost double.

Heat oven to 400°. Spray top of loaf with water. Bake 10 minutes, spraying 3 times with water. Bake 15 to 20 minutes longer or until loaf is golden brown and sounds hollow when tapped. Remove from cookie sheet to wire rack; cool.

■ 1 Slice: 175 calories (10 calories from fat); 1g fat (0g saturated); 0mg cholesterol; 210mg sodium; 37g carbohydrate (1g dietary fiber); 5g protein

Challah

1 loaf, 12 slices

3/4 cup plus 1 tablespoon water

1 egg

2 tablespoons margarine or butter, softened

3 1/4 cups bread flour

2 tablespoons sugar

1 1/2 teaspoons salt

1 1/2 teaspoons bread machine or quick active dry yeast

1 egg yolk

2 tablespoons cold water

1 tablespoon poppy seed

Measure carefully, placing all ingredients except egg yolk, cold water and poppy seed in bread machine pan in the order recommended by the manufacturer.

Select Dough/Manual cycle. Do not use delay cycles.

Remove dough from pan, using lightly floured hands. Cover and let rest 10 minutes on lightly floured surface.

Grease large cookie sheet. Divide dough into thirds. Roll each third into 13-inch rope. Braid ropes gently and loosely, starting at the middle. Pinch ends to seal; tuck ends under braid. Place on cookie sheet. Cover and let rise in warm place about 45 minutes or until double. (Dough is ready if indentation remains when touched.)

Heat oven to 375°. Mix egg yolk and cold water; brush over loaf. Sprinkle with poppy seed. Bake about 25 minutes or until golden brown.

■ 1 Slice: 165 calories (25 calories from fat); 3g fat (1g saturated); 35mg cholesterol; 330mg sodium; 31g carbohydrate (1g dietary fiber); 5g protein

SUCCESS TIP

To keep that pretty braid shape, be careful not to stretch the dough as you are making the braid. Also, starting in the middle will help prevent the dough from stretching.

DID YOU KNOW?

Challah (pronounced KHAH-lah) is a traditional Jewish yeast bread served for everyday meals as well as special holidays and Sabbath. The braid is the classic shape for this rich, tender dough, but it can be formed into other shapes. No matter what shape or form, it still tastes delicious!

SHAPING

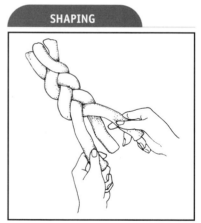

Braid ropes gently and loosely, starting at the middle.

French Baguettes

2 baguettes, 12 slices each

DO-AHEAD NOTE

Cover slashed loaves with plastic wrap. Refrigerate from 4 hours up to 48 hours. Before baking, remove the plastic wrap, cover with kitchen towel and let rise in a warm place about 2 hours or until it is almost double. Brush the tops and bake as the recipe tells you.

SHAPING

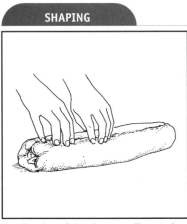

Pinch edge of dough into roll to seal.

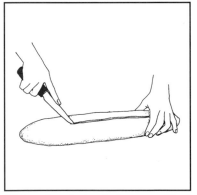

Make a lengthwise slash on top of loaf.

1 cup water

2 3/4 cups bread flour

1 tablespoon sugar

1 teaspoon salt

1 1/2 teaspoons bread machine or quick active dry yeast

1 egg yolk

1 tablespoon water

Measure carefully, placing all ingredients except egg yolk and 1 table-spoon water in bread machine pan in the order recommended by the manufacturer.

Select Dough/Manual cycle. Do not use delay cycles.

Remove dough from pan, using lightly floured hands. Place dough in greased bowl, turning to coat all sides. Cover and let rise in warm place about 30 minutes or until double. (Dough is ready if indentation remains when touched.)

Grease cookie sheet. Punch down dough. Roll dough into 16 × 12-inch rectangle on lightly floured surface. Cut dough crosswise in half to make two 8 × 12 pieces. Roll up each half of dough tightly, beginning at 12-inch side. Pinch edge of dough into roll to seal. Gently roll back and forth to taper ends.

Place loaves 3 inches apart on cookie sheet. Make 3 or 4 diagonal slashes across tops of loaves, using sharp knife, or make 1 lengthwise slash on each loaf. Cover and let rise in warm place 30 to 40 minutes or until double.

Heat oven to 375°. Mix egg yolk and 1 tablespoon water; brush over tops of loaves. Bake 20 to 25 minutes or until golden brown. Serve warm, or cool on wire rack.

■ 1 Slice: 60 calories (0 calories from fat); 0g fat (0g saturated); 10mg cholesterol; 100mg sodium; 13g carbohydrate (0g dietary fiber); 2g protein

Roasted Pepper and Artichoke Baguette

2 baguettes, 12 slices each

1/2 cup water

1/2 cup roasted red bell peppers (from 12-ounce jar), drained and chopped (see Note below)

1/3 cup marinated artichoke hearts (from 6-ounce jar), well drained

1 tablespoon margarine or butter, softened

3 1/4 cups bread flour

1 tablespoon sugar

1 teaspoon garlic powder

3/4 teaspoon salt

1 1/2 teaspoons bread machine or quick active dry yeast

1 egg, slightly beaten

Measure carefully, placing all ingredients except egg in bread machine pan in the order recommended by the manufacturer.

Select Dough/Manual cycle. Do not use delay cycles.

Remove dough from pan, using lightly floured hands. Knead 10 times on lightly floured surface. Cover and let rest 10 minutes.

Grease large cookie sheet. Roll dough into 16 × 12-inch rectangle on lightly floured surface. Cut dough crosswise in half to make two 8 × 12 pieces. Roll up each half tightly, beginning at 12-inch side. Pinch edge of dough into roll to seal. Gently roll back and forth to taper ends.

Place loaves 3 inches apart on cookie sheet. Make 3 or 4 diagonal slashes across tops of loaves, using sharp knife, or make 1 lengthwise slash on each loaf. Cover and let rise in warm place 30 to 40 minutes or until double. (Dough is ready if indentation remains when touched.)

Heat oven to 375°. Brush egg over tops of loaves. Bake 20 to 25 minutes or until golden brown. Serve warm, or cool on wire rack.

■ 1 Slice: 75 calories (10 calories from fat); 1g fat (0g saturated); 10mg cholesterol; 90mg sodium; 15g carbohydrate (1g dietary fiber); 2g protein

NOTE: You can roast your own bell peppers for this recipe. Broil whole peppers about 5 inches from the heat, turning them often, until the skins are blistered and an even deep brown. Place the hot peppers in a paper bag or wrap them in a kitchen towel, and let stand about 20 minutes. The skins will easily slip off the peppers.

DO-AHEAD NOTE

After you have patted the dough into a rectangle on the cookie sheet, cover it with plastic wrap. You can refrigerate it from 4 hours up to 48 hours. Before baking, remove the dough from the refrigerator and remove plastic wrap. Cover with kitchen towel and let rise in a warm place about 2 hours or until it is almost double. Then continue as the recipe tells you.

SHAPING

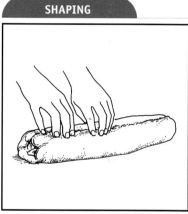

Pinch edge of dough into roll to seal.

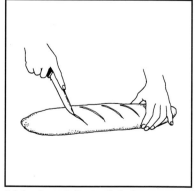

Make 3 or 4 diagonal slashes on top of loaf.

Zesty Pesto Tomato Baguettes

2 baguettes, 8 slices each

SUCCESS TIP

If your bread machine doesn't have a Raisin/Nut signal, add the tomatoes 5 to 10 minutes before the last kneading cycle ends. Check your bread machine's use-and-care book out for how long the last cycle runs.

SHAPING

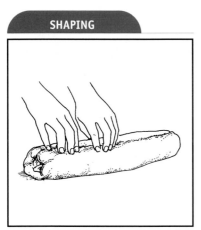

Pinch edge of dough into roll to seal.

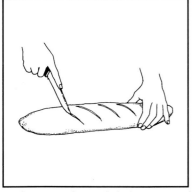

Make 3 or 4 diagonal slashes on top of loaf.

1 cup plus 2 tablespoons water

1/3 cup pesto

3 cups bread flour

2 tablespoons sugar

1 1/2 teaspoons salt

1 1/4 teaspoons bread machine or quick active dry yeast

1/3 cup coarsely chopped sun-dried tomatoes (packed in oil), drained

1 egg, beaten

Shredded Asiago or Parmesan cheese, if desired

Measure carefully, placing all ingredients except tomatoes, egg and cheese in bread machine pan in the order recommended by the manufacturer. Add tomatoes at the Raisin/Nut signal.

Select Dough/Manual cycle. Do not use delay cycles.

Remove dough from pan, using lightly floured hands. Cover and let rest 10 minutes on lightly floured surface.

Grease large cookie sheet. Roll dough into 16 × 12-inch rectangle on lightly floured surface. Cut dough crosswise in half. Roll up each half of dough tightly, beginning at 12-inch side. Pinch edge of dough into roll to seal. Gently roll back and forth to taper ends.

Place loaves 3 inches apart on cookie sheet. Make 3 or 4 diagonal slashes across tops of loaves, using sharp knife, or make 1 lengthwise slash on each loaf. Cover and let rise in warm place 30 to 40 minutes or until double. (Dough is ready if indentation remains when touched.)

Heat oven to 375°. Brush egg over tops of loaves. Sprinkle with cheese. Bake 20 to 25 minutes or until golden brown. Serve warm, or cool on wire rack.

■ 1 Slice: 115 calories (30 calories from fat); 4g fat (1g saturated); 1mg cholesterol; 250mg sodium; 20g carbohydrate (1g dietary fiber); 3g protein

DO-AHEAD NOTE: Cover slashed loaves with plastic wrap. Refrigerate them 4 hours up to 48 hours. Before baking, remove plastic wrap, cover with kitchen towel and let rise in a warm place about 2 hours or until it is almost double. Brush with egg, sprinkle with cheese and bake.

Zesty Pesto Tomato Baguettes

Italian Artichoke Braid

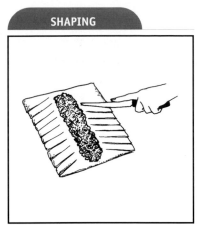

Make cuts from filling to edge of dough at 1-inch intervals.

Fold strips over filling, alternating sides and overlapping at center.

1 braid, 12 slices

2/3 cup water

1 tablespoon olive or vegetable oil

2 1/4 cups bread flour

2 teaspoons Italian seasoning (see Note below)

3/4 teaspoon salt

2 teaspoons bread machine or quick active dry yeast

Artichoke Filling (below)

1 cup shredded provolone cheese (4 ounces)

Measure carefully, placing all ingredients except Artichoke Filling and cheese in bread machine pan in the order recommended by the manufacturer.

Select Dough/Manual cycle. Do not use delay cycles.

Remove dough from pan. Knead 5 minutes on lightly floured surface (if necessary, knead in enough flour to make dough easy to handle). Cover and let rest 10 minutes. Prepare Artichoke Filling.

Grease large cookie sheet. Roll dough into 12 × 8-inch rectangle. Place on cookie sheet. Spoon filling lengthwise down center third of rectangle; sprinkle with cheese. On each 12-inch side, make cuts from filling to edge of dough at 1-inch intervals, using sharp knife. Fold ends up over filling. Fold strips diagonally over filling, alternating sides and overlapping in center. Cover and let rise in warm place 20 to 40 minutes or until double. (Dough is ready if indentation remains when touched.)

Heat oven to 400°. Bake 20 to 25 minutes or until golden brown. Serve warm, or cool on wire rack.

Artichoke Filling

1 jar (6 ounces) quartered marinated artichoke hearts, drained and chopped

1/3 cup sliced ripe olives

1/3 cup roasted red bell peppers (from 7-ounce jar), drained and chopped

Mix all ingredients.

■ 1 Slice: 155 calories (45 calories from fat); 5g fat (2g saturated); 10mg cholesterol; 300mg sodium; 22g carbohydrate (1g dietary fiber); 6g protein

NOTE: If Italian seasoning isn't a blend you keep on your shelf, use 1 teaspoon dried basil, 1/2 teaspoon dried oregano, 1/4 teaspoon dried rosemary, 1/4 teaspoon garlic powder and a dash of ground red pepper (cayenne) instead.

Rosemary Focaccia

1 focaccia, 8 servings

3/4 cup water

2 tablespoons olive or vegetable oil

2 cups bread flour

1 tablespoon sugar

1 teaspoon salt

1 1/2 teaspoons bread machine or quick active dry yeast

3 tablespoons olive or vegetable oil

2 to 3 tablespoons chopped fresh rosemary leaves

Coarse salt, if desired

Measure carefully, placing all ingredients except 3 tablespoons oil, the rosemary and coarse salt in bread machine pan in the order recommended by the manufacturer.

Select Dough/Manual cycle. Do not use delay cycles.

Remove dough from pan, using lightly floured hands. Cover and let rest on lightly floured surface 10 minutes.

Grease large cookie sheet. Roll or pat dough into 12-inch circle on cookie sheet. Cover and let rise in warm place about 30 minutes or until almost double.

Heat oven to 400°. Make depressions in dough at 1-inch intervals with fingertips. Drizzle with 3 tablespoons oil. Sprinkle with rosemary and coarse salt. Bake 15 to 18 minutes or until golden brown. Serve warm, or cool on wire rack.

■ 1 Serving: 205 calories (80 calories from fat); 9g fat (1g saturated); 0mg cholesterol; 270mg sodium; 28g carbohydrate (1g dietary fiber); 4g protein

SUCCESS TIP

Be sure to chop the rosemary leaves instead of leaving them whole. They can become dry quickly during baking, which makes them sharper and can be unsafe to swallow.

DO-AHEAD NOTE

After you have patted the dough into a circle on the cookie sheet, cover it with plastic wrap. You can refrigerate it from 4 hours up to 48 hours. Before baking, remove the dough from the refrigerator and remove plastic wrap. Cover with kitchen towel and let rise in a warm place about 2 hours or until it is almost double. Then continue as the recipe tells you.

SHAPING

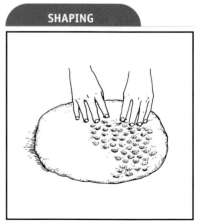

Make depressions in dough at 1-inch intervals with fingertips.

Greek Olive Focaccia

1 focaccia, 8 servings

3/4 cup water

1 small onion, chopped (1/4 cup)

2 tablespoons olive or vegetable oil

3 cups bread flour

2 tablespoons sugar

1 teaspoon salt

1 teaspoon dried rosemary leaves

1 3/4 teaspoons bread machine or quick active dry yeast

1/3 cup Kalamata or Greek olives, pitted

1 tablespoon olive or vegetable oil

1 teaspoon dried rosemary leaves, if desired

Measure carefully, placing all ingredients except olives, 1 tablespoon oil and 1 teaspoon rosemary in bread machine pan in the order recommended by the manufacturer. Add olives at the Raisin/Nut signal.

Select Dough/Manual cycle. Do not use delay cycles.

Remove dough from pan, using lightly floured hands. Cover and let rest 10 minutes on lightly floured surface.

Grease cookie sheet. Pat dough into 12-inch circle on cookie sheet. Cover and let rise in warm place about 30 minutes or until almost double.

Heat oven to 400°. Make deep depressions in dough at 1-inch intervals with fingertips. Drizzle with 1 tablespoon oil. Sprinkle with 1 teaspoon rosemary. Bake 15 to 18 minutes or until edge is golden brown. Serve warm, or cool on wire rack.

■ 1 Serving: 235 calories (45 calories from fat); 5g fat (1g saturated); 0mg cholesterol; 340mg sodium; 43g carbohydrate (2g dietary fiber); 6g protein

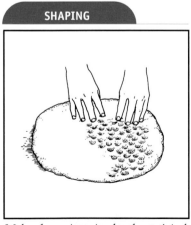

Make depressions in dough at 1-inch intervals with fingertips.

Roasted Pepper Focaccia

1 focaccia, 12 servings

1 cup water

1 tablespoon margarine or butter, softened

3 cups bread flour

1 tablespoon sugar

1 teaspoon garlic powder

3/4 teaspoon salt

1 1/2 teaspoons bread machine yeast or quick active dry yeast

1/2 cup roasted red bell peppers (from 12-ounce jar), drained and chopped

1/3 cup quartered marinated artichoke hearts (from 6-ounce jar), drained

Cornmeal

1 tablespoon olive or vegetable oil

Coarse salt, if desired

Measure carefully, placing all ingredients except bell peppers, artichokes, cornmeal, oil and coarse salt in bread machine pan in the order recommended by the manufacturer. Add bell peppers and artichokes at the Raisin/Nut signal.

Select Dough/Manual cycle. Do not use delay cycles.

Remove dough from pan, using lightly floured hands. Cover and let rest 10 minutes on lightly floured surface.

Grease large cookie sheet; sprinkle with cornmeal. Pat dough into 15 × 12-inch rectangle on cookie sheet. Cover and let rise in warm place 35 to 40 minutes or until almost double.

Heat oven to 400°. Make deep depressions in dough at 1-inch intervals with fingertips. Drizzle or brush with oil. Sprinkle with coarse salt. Bake 18 to 20 minutes or until golden brown. Serve warm, or cool on wire rack.

■ 1 Serving: 135 calories (10 calories from fat); 1g fat (0g saturated); 0mg cholesterol; 180mg sodium; 28g carbohydrate (1g dietary fiber); 4g protein

SUCCESS TIP

If your bread machine doesn't have a Raisin/Nut signal, add the bell peppers and artichokes 5 to 10 minutes before the last kneading cycle ends. Check your bread machine's use-and-care book to find out how long the last cycle runs.

DO-AHEAD NOTE

After you have patted the dough into a rectangle on the cookie sheet, cover it with plastic wrap. You can refrigerate it from 4 hours up to 48 hours. Before baking, Remove the dough from the refrigerator and Remove plastic wrap. Cover with kitchen towel and let rise in a warm place about 2 hours or until it is almost double. Then continue as the recipe tells you.

SHAPING

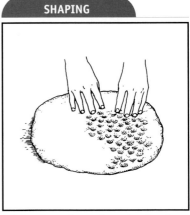

Make deep depressions in dough at 1-inch intervals with fingertips.

Crusty Mustard Focaccia

DO-AHEAD NOTE

After you have patted the dough into a circle on the cookie sheet, cover it with plastic wrap. You can refrigerate it from 4 hours up to 48 hours. Before baking, remove the dough from the refrigerator and remove plastic wrap. Cover with kitchen towel and let rise in a warm place about 2 hours or until it is almost double. Then continue as the recipe tells you.

DID YOU KNOW?

Prepared mustard generally is made from powdered mustard, which is finely ground mustard seed, and combined with seasonings and liquid such as water, vinegar, wine or beer. Prepared spicy mustard can range from hot to mild to sweet—use the variety that you like best.

SHAPING

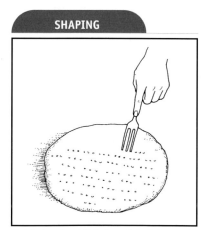

Prick dough with fork at 1-inch intervals.

1 focaccia, 8 servings

2/3 cup water

1 tablespoon olive or vegetable oil

2 tablespoons spicy mustard

2 1/4 cups bread flour

1 tablespoon sugar

1 teaspoon salt

1 1/2 teaspoons bread machine or quick active dry yeast

3 tablespoons olive or vegetable oil

Coarse salt, if desired

Measure carefully, placing all ingredients except 3 tablespoons oil and the coarse salt in bread machine pan in the order recommended by the manufacturer.

Select Dough/Manual cycle. Do not use delay cycles.

Remove dough from pan, using lightly floured hands. Knead 5 minutes on lightly floured surface (if necessary, knead in enough flour to make dough easy to handle). Cover and let rest 10 minutes.

Grease large cookie sheet. Roll or pat dough into 12-inch circle on cookie sheet. Cover and let rise in warm place about 10 minutes or until almost double.

Heat oven to 400°. Prick dough with fork at 1-inch intervals or make deep depressions in dough with fingertips. Brush with 3 tablespoons oil. Sprinkle with coarse salt. Bake 15 to 18 minutes or until golden brown. Serve warm, or cool on wire rack.

■ 1 Serving: 160 calories (20 calories from fat); 2g fat (0g saturated); 0mg cholesterol; 340mg sodium; 32g carbohydrate (1g dietary fiber); 4g protein

Two-Cheese Pizza

1 pizza, 8 wedges

1/2 cup water

1 tablespoon vegetable oil

1 1/2 cups bread flour

1/2 teaspoon Italian seasoning, if desired

1/2 teaspoon salt

1/4 teaspoon sugar

1 1/4 teaspoons bread machine or quick active dry yeast

3/4 cup pizza sauce

1 1/2 cups shredded mozzarella cheese (6 ounces)

1/4 cup shredded Parmesan cheese

Measure carefully, placing all ingredients except pizza sauce and cheeses in bread machine pan in the order recommended by the manufacturer.

Select Dough/Manual cycle. Do not use delay cycles.

Remove dough from pan, using lightly floured hands. Knead 5 minutes on lightly floured surface (if necessary, knead in enough flour to make dough easy to handle). Cover and let rest 10 minutes.

Move oven rack to lowest position. Heat oven to 450°. Grease large cookie sheet or 12-inch pizza pan. Pat dough into 13-inch circle on cookie sheet; pinch edge, forming 1/2-inch rim. Spread pizza sauce over dough. Sprinkle with cheeses. Bake 12 to 15 minutes or until crust is golden brown and cheeses are melted.

■ 1 Wedge: 175 calories (55 calories from fat); 6g fat (3g saturated); 15mg cholesterol; 410mg sodium; 22g carbohydrate (1g dietary fiber); 10g protein

Mexican Beef Pizza

1 pizza, 8 wedges

1/2 cup water

1 tablespoon vegetable oil

1 1/2 cups bread flour

1/2 teaspoon salt

1/4 teaspoon sugar

1 1/4 teaspoons bread machine or quick active dry yeast

Mexican Beef Topping (below)

3/4 cup shredded Monterey Jack or Cheddar cheese (3 ounces)

Measure all ingredients except Mexican Beef Topping and cheese in bread machine pan in the order recommended by the manufacturer.

Select Dough/Manual cycle. Do not use delay cycles.

Remove dough from pan. Knead 5 minutes on lightly floured surface (if necessary, knead in enough flour to make dough easy to handle). Cover and let rest 10 minutes. Prepare Mexican Beef Topping.

Move oven rack to lowest position. Heat oven to 450°. Grease large cookie sheet or 12-inch pizza pan. Pat dough into 13-inch circle on cookie sheet; pinch edge, forming 1/2-inch rim. Spread topping over dough. Sprinkle with cheese. Bake 12 to 15 minutes or until crust is golden brown and cheese is melted.

DO-AHEAD NOTE

After you have patted the dough into a circle on the cookie sheet, cover it with plastic wrap. You can refrigerate it from 4 hours up to 48 hours. Before baking, remove the dough from the refrigerator and remove plastic wrap. Cover with kitchen towel and let rise in a warm place about 2 hours or until it is almost double. Make the beef topping, and bake your pizza as the recipe tells you.

TRY THIS

If you'd like this Mexican pizza hotter, try using chopped jalapeño, Fresno or habanero. A general rule is the smaller the chili, the hotter the flavor.

Mexican Beef Topping

1/2 pound ground beef

1/3 cup chopped onion

1/2 teaspoon dried oregano leaves

1 teaspoon chili powder

1/2 teaspoon garlic salt

1/4 teaspoon pepper

3/4 cup shredded Monterey Jack or Cheddar cheese (3 ounces)

1 can (28 ounces) whole tomatoes, drained and chopped

1 can (4 ounces) chopped green chilies, drained

Cook beef, onion, oregano, chili powder, garlic salt and pepper in 10-inch skillet over medium heat, stirring occasionally, until beef is brown; drain. Stir in remaining ingredients.

■ 1 Wedge: 270 calories (115 calories from fat); 13g fat (6g saturated); 36mg cholesterol; 530mg sodium; 26g carbohydrate (2g dietary fiber); 14g protein

Chicken Fajita Pizza

1 pizza, 8 wedges

1/2 cup water

1 tablespoon vegetable oil

1 1/2 cups bread flour

2 teaspoons chopped fresh or 1 1/2 teaspoons dried cilantro, if desired

1/2 teaspoon salt

1/4 teaspoon sugar

1 1/4 teaspoons bread machine or quick active dry yeast

Chicken Fajita Topping (below)

1 1/2 cups shredded Monterey Jack or Cheddar cheese (6 ounces)

Measure carefully, placing all ingredients except Chicken Fajita Topping and cheese in bread machine pan in the order recommended by the manufacturer.

Select Dough/Manual cycle. Do not use delay cycles.

Remove dough from pan, using lightly floured hands. Knead 5 minutes on lightly floured surface (if necessary, knead in enough flour to make dough easy to handle). Cover and let rest 10 minutes. Prepare Chicken Fajita Topping.

Move oven rack to lowest position. Heat oven to 450°. Grease large cookie sheet or 12-inch pizza pan. Pat dough into 13-inch circle on cookie sheet; pinch edge, forming 1/2-inch rim. Spread topping over dough. Sprinkle with cheese. Bake 12 to 15 minutes or until crust is golden brown and cheese is melted.

Chicken Fajita Topping

1/2 pound boneless, skinless chicken breast halves

1 tablespoon vegetable oil

1 medium bell pepper, cut into thin rings

1 small onion, sliced

1 cup salsa

Cut chicken into strips, 1/8 to 1/4 inch thick. Heat oil in 10-inch skillet over medium-high heat. Cook chicken in oil 3 minutes, stirring occasionally. Stir in bell pepper and onion. Cook 3 to 4 minutes, stirring occasionally, until chicken is no longer pink in center and vegetables are crisp-tender; remove from heat. Stir in salsa.

■ 1 Wedge: 240 calories (100 calories from fat); 11g fat (5g saturated); 35mg cholesterol; 380mg sodium; 23g carbohydrate (2g dietary fiber); 14g protein

Mediterranean Peppered Pizza

1 pizza, 8 wedges

1/2 cup water

1 tablespoon vegetable oil

1 1/2 cups bread flour

1/2 teaspoon salt

1/4 teaspoon sugar

1 1/4 teaspoons bread machine or quick active dry yeast

Mediterranean Peppered Topping (below)

1 1/2 cups shredded mozzarella cheese (6 ounces)

2 roma (plum) tomatoes or 1 small tomato, sliced

Measure carefully, placing all ingredients except Mediterranean Peppered Topping, cheese and tomatoes in bread machine pan in the order recommended by the manufacturer.

Select Dough/Manual cycle. Do not use delay cycles.

Remove dough from pan. Knead 5 minutes on lightly floured surface (if necessary, knead in flour to make dough easy to handle). Cover and let rest 10 minutes. Prepare Mediterranean Peppered Topping.

Move oven rack to lowest position. Heat oven to 450°. Grease large cookie sheet or 12-inch pizza pan. Pat dough into 13-inch circle on cookie sheet; pinch edge, forming 1/2-inch rim. Sprinkle 3/4 cup of the cheese over dough. Spoon topping onto cheese. Sprinkle remaining 3/4 cup cheese over topping; arrange tomatoes on top. Bake 12 to 15 minutes or until crust is golden brown and cheese is melted.

DO-AHEAD NOTE

After you have patted the dough into a circle on the cookie sheet, cover it with plastic wrap. You can refrigerate it from 4 hours up to 48 hours. Before baking, remove the dough from the refrigerator and remove plastic wrap. Cover with kitchen towel and let rise in a warm place about 2 hours or until it is almost double. Make the peppered topping, and bake your pizza as the recipe tells you.

DID YOU KNOW?

Pepperoncini (pronounced pep-per-awn-CHEE-nee) is a thin, bright red, wrinkled-skin chili about 2 to 3 inches long. Also called Tuscan pepper, it has a slightly sweet flavor that ranges from medium to medium-hot. You can use other pickled chilies for this pizza.

Mediterranean Peppered Topping

1 jar (7 ounces) roasted red bell peppers, drained and chopped (3/4 cup)

1 jar (7 ounces) sun-dried tomatoes in oil, drained and chopped

2 pepperoncini peppers (bottled Italian peppers), drained and sliced

1 can (2 1/4 ounces) sliced ripe olives, drained

1 small onion, finely chopped (1/4 cup)

1 tablespoon chopped fresh basil leaves

Mix all ingredients.

■ 1 Wedge: 240 calories (90 calories from fat); 10g fat (3g saturated); 10mg cholesterol; 410mg sodium; 30g carbohydrate (3g dietary fiber); 10g protein

Satisfying Rolls and Breadsticks

Bagels (page 184)

Dinner Rolls

15 rolls

1 cup water

2 tablespoons margarine or butter, softened

1 egg

3 1/4 cups bread flour

1/4 cup sugar

1 teaspoon salt

3 teaspoons bread machine or quick active dry yeast

Margarine or butter, melted, if desired

Measure carefully, placing all ingredients except melted margarine in bread machine pan in the order recommended by the manufacturer.

Select Dough/Manual cycle. Do not use delay cycles.

Remove dough from pan, using lightly floured hands. Cover and let rest 10 minutes on lightly floured surface.

Grease large cookie sheet. Divide dough into 15 equal pieces. Shape each piece into a ball. Place 2 inches apart on cookie sheet. Cover and let rise in warm place 30 to 40 minutes or until double. (Dough is ready if indentation remains when touched.)

Heat oven to 375°. Bake 12 to 15 minutes or until golden brown. Brush tops with melted margarine. Serve warm, or cool on wire rack.

■ 1 Roll: 135 calories (20 calories from fat); 2g fat (0g saturated); 15mg cholesterol; 170mg sodium; 26g carbohydrate (1g dietary fiber); 4g protein

Whole Wheat Dinner Rolls

12 rolls

3/4 cup water

1 tablespoon shortening

1 1/4 cups bread flour

1 cup whole wheat flour

2 tablespoons packed brown sugar

1 tablespoon dry milk

1/2 teaspoon salt

1 1/4 teaspoons bread machine or quick active dry yeast

Margarine or butter, melted

Measure carefully, placing all ingredients except margarine in bread machine pan in the order recommended by the manufacturer.

Select Dough/Manual cycle. Do not use delay cycles.

Remove dough from pan, using lightly floured hands. Knead 5 minutes on lightly floured surface. Cover and let rest 10 minutes.

Grease large cookie sheet. Divide dough into 12 equal pieces. Shape each piece into a ball. Place 2 inches apart on cookie sheet. Brush with margarine. Cover and let rise in warm place 30 to 40 minutes or until double. (Dough is ready if indentation remains when touched.)

Heat oven to 375°. Bake 15 to 20 minutes or until golden brown. Serve warm, or cool on wire rack.

■ 1 Roll: 135 calories (45 calories from fat); 5g fat (1g saturated); 0mg cholesterol; 150mg sodium; 21g carbohydrate (2g dietary fiber); 3g protein

SUCCESS TIP

We have kneaded the dough after it comes out of the bread machine to help develop the gluten, so the rolls have a nice, light texture. If the dough tends to spring back into place even after letting it rest 10 minutes, cover it again and let it rest another 5 minutes.

DO-AHEAD NOTE

After you have shaped the dough into rolls and placed them on the cookie sheet, cover with plastic wrap. You can refrigerate them from 4 hours up to 48 hours. Before baking, remove the rolls from the refrigerator and remove plastic wrap. Cover with kitchen towel and let rise in a warm place about 2 hours or until double. Bake the rolls as the recipe tells you.

Whole Wheat Buttermilk Rolls

SUCCESS TIP

We found that letting the dough rise twice—once in the bowl, then again after shaping the rolls—gave these heavenly whole wheat rolls a lighter, more tender texture.

DO-AHEAD NOTE

After you have shaped the dough into rolls and placed them on the cookie sheet, cover with plastic wrap. You can refrigerate them from 4 hours up to 48 hours. Before baking, remove the rolls from the refrigerator and remove plastic wrap. Cover with kitchen towel and let rise in a warm place about 2 hours or until double. Bake the rolls as the recipe tells you.

TRY THIS

For an added hint of honey, brush the hot baked rolls with honey that has been heated. This also adds a nice glaze to the top of the rolls.

24 rolls

1 1/2 cups buttermilk

1/4 cup shortening

2 tablespoons honey

2 cups whole wheat flour

1 1/4 cups bread flour

1/2 cup wheat germ

1 1/2 teaspoons salt

2 teaspoons bread machine or quick active dry yeast

3 tablespoons margarine or butter, melted

Measure carefully, placing all ingredients except margarine in bread machine pan in the order recommended by the manufacturer.

Select Dough/Manual cycle. Do not use delay cycles.

Remove dough from pan, using lightly floured hands. Place dough in greased bowl, and turn greased side up. Cover and let rise in warm place about 30 minutes or until double. (Dough is ready if indentation remains when touched.)

Grease large cookie sheet. Punch down dough. Place dough on lightly floured surface. Divide dough into 24 equal pieces. Shape each piece into a ball. Place slightly apart on cookie sheet. Cover and let rise about 30 minutes or until double. Brush with margarine.

Heat oven to 350°. Bake 15 to 20 minutes or until golden brown. Serve warm, or cool on wire rack.

■ 1 Roll: 105 calories (35 calories from fat); 4g fat (1g saturated); 0mg cholesterol; 170mg sodium; 16g carbohydrate (2g dietary fiber); 3g protein

Crescent Rolls

20 rolls

1 egg, slightly beaten, plus enough water to equal 1 1/3 cups

1 cup margarine or butter, softened

1 1/2 teaspoons salt

1/4 cup sugar

4 cups bread flour

2 teaspoons bread machine or quick active dry yeast

2 tablespoons margarine or butter, melted

Measure carefully, placing all ingredients except 2 tablespoons melted margarine in bread machine pan in the order recommended by the manufacturer.

Select Dough/Manual cycle. Do not use delay cycles.

Remove dough from pan, using lightly floured hands. Place dough in greased bowl, and turn greased side up. Cover and let rise in warm place about 30 minutes or until double. (Dough is ready if indentation remains when touched.)

Grease cookie sheet. Punch down dough. Roll dough into 20-inch circle on lightly floured surface. Brush with some of the melted margarine. Cut into 20 wedges. Roll up each wedge, beginning at rounded edge. Place rolls, point sides down, on cookie sheet and curve slightly. Cover and let rise in warm place 20 to 30 minutes or until almost double.

Heat oven to 375°. Brush rolls with remaining melted margarine. Bake 8 to 10 minutes or until golden brown. Serve warm, or cool on rack.

■ 1 Roll: 195 calories (90 calories from fat); 10g fat (2g saturated); 10mg cholesterol; 280mg sodium; 24g carbohydrate (1g dietary fiber); 3g protein

DO-AHEAD NOTE: After you have shaped the dough into rolls and placed them on the cookie sheet, cover with plastic wrap. You can refrigerate them from 4 hours up to 48 hours. Before baking, remove the rolls from the refrigerator and remove plastic wrap. Cover with kitchen towel and let rise in a warm place about 2 hours or until double. Bake the rolls as the recipe tells you above.

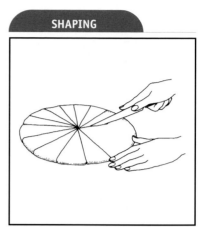

Roll dough into 20-inch circle and cut into 20 wedges.

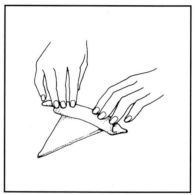

Roll up each wedge, beginning at rounded edge.

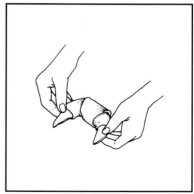

Place rolls, point side down, on cookie sheet and curve slightly.

Curry Rice Dinner Rolls

10 rolls

2/3 cup water

1 tablespoon vegetable oil

2 cups bread flour

1/2 cup cooked brown rice

1 teaspoon salt

3/4 teaspoon sugar

1/2 teaspoon curry powder

1 teaspoon bread machine or quick active dry yeast

Margarine or butter, melted

Measure carefully, placing all ingredients except margarine in bread machine pan in the order recommended by the manufacturer.

Select Dough/Manual cycle. Do not use delay cycles.

Remove dough from pan, using lightly floured hands. Knead 5 minutes on lightly floured surface. Cover and let rest 10 minutes.

Grease large cookie sheet. Divide dough into 10 equal pieces. Shape each piece into a ball. Place 2 inches apart on cookie sheet. Brush with margarine. Cover and let rise in warm place 30 to 40 minutes or until double. (Dough is ready if indentation remains when touched.)

Heat oven to 375°. Bake 15 to 20 minutes or until golden brown. Serve warm, or cool on wire rack.

■ 1 Roll: 160 calories (55 calories from fat); 6g fat (1g saturated); 0mg cholesterol; 280mg sodium; 24g carbohydrate (1g dietary fiber); 3g protein

SUCCESS TIP

We found that we had better results when using cold or room-temperature rice instead of hot cooked rice. Cook the brown rice ahead and cool to room temperature or refrigerate. To cool the rice quickly, spread it out on a cookie sheet or large plate before you refrigerate it. This recipe is also a good way to use any leftover rice you might have on hand.

DO-AHEAD NOTE

After you have shaped the dough into rolls and placed them on the cookie sheet, cover with plastic wrap. You can refrigerate them from 4 hours up to 48 hours. Before baking, remove the rolls from the refrigerator and remove plastic wrap. Cover with kitchen towel and let rise in a warm place about 2 hours or until double. Bake the rolls as the recipe tells you.

DID YOU KNOW?

Brown rice is the entire grain with only the inedible outer husk removed. This light tan-colored rice has a nutlike flavor and slightly chewy texture. Because it still has the bran, it can become rancid, so plan to keep it on your shelf for about six months. If you don't have brown rice, you can use regular cooked white rice for these rolls.

Curry Rice Dinner Rolls

Raisin Brioche

12 rolls

1/4 cup milk

3 tablespoons water

1/3 cup margarine or butter, softened

2 egg yolks

2 cups bread flour

1/3 cup sugar

1 teaspoon ground cinnamon

1/2 teaspoon salt

3 teaspoons bread machine or quick active dry yeast

1 cup golden raisins (see Note below)

1 egg, beaten

Measure carefully, placing all ingredients except raisins and beaten egg in bread machine pan in the order recommended by the manufacturer. Add raisins at the Raisin/Nut signal.

Select Dough/Manual cycle. Do not use delay cycles.

Remove dough from pan, using lightly floured hands. Cover and let rest 10 minutes on lightly floured surface.

Grease 12 large muffin cups, 3 × 1 1/2 inches. Divide dough into 16 equal pieces. Shape each piece into a ball, using floured hands. Cut 4 balls into 3 pieces each; roll into small balls. Place 12 large balls in muffin cups. Make indentation in center of each large ball with thumb. Place 1 small ball in each indentation. Cover and refrigerate 2 hours.

Remove rolls from refrigerator. Let rise covered in warm place 40 to 45 minutes or until almost double.

Heat oven to 350°. Brush beaten egg over rolls. Bake 22 to 26 minutes or until golden brown. Immediately remove from pan. Serve warm, or cool on wire rack.

■ 1 Roll: 205 calories (65 calories from fat); 7g fat (2g saturated); 55mg cholesterol; 180mg sodium; 33g carbohydrate (1g dietary fiber); 4g protein

NOTE: If your bread machine doesn't have a Raisin/Nut signal, add the raisins 5 to 10 minutes before the last kneading cycle ends. Check your bread machine's use-and-care book for how long the last cycle runs.

Raisin Brioche

SHAPING

Cut 4 balls into 3 pieces each; roll each piece into a small cone-shaped ball.

Make indentation in center of each large ball with finger.

Place 1 small ball in each indentation.

Bagels

SUCCESS TIP

Boil only 3 or 4 bagels at one time so they have room to "swim" in the boiling water rather than sticking together. Work quickly, and don't let the boiled bagels drain too long on the paper towels because they may begin to stick to the paper.

SHAPING

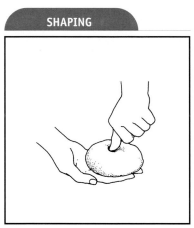

Shape each piece into 3-inch circle; poke 1-inch hole in center, using thumb.

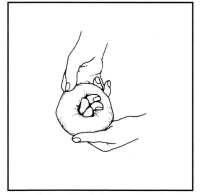

Smooth into bagel shape, using fingers.

10 bagels

1 cup plus 1 tablespoon water

1 1/2 tablespoons honey

3 cups bread flour

1 1/4 teaspoons salt

1 1/2 teaspoons bread machine or quick active dry yeast

Old-fashioned oats, instant minced onion, sesame seed or poppy seed, if desired

Measure carefully, placing all ingredients except oats in bread machine pan in the order recommended by the manufacturer.

Select Dough/Manual cycle. Do not use delay cycles. Stop cycle after 50 minutes; remove dough from pan, using lightly floured hands.

Grease cookie sheet. Cut dough into 10 equal pieces. Shape each piece into 3-inch circle; poke 1-inch hole in center, using thumbs. Smooth into bagel shape, using fingers. Place on cookie sheet. Cover and let rise in warm place about 20 minutes or until almost double.

Heat oven to 450°. Heat 2 quarts water to boiling in Dutch oven. Lower 3 or 4 bagels at a time into boiling water. Boil 30 seconds, turning once after 15 seconds. Remove with slotted spoon; drain on paper towels. Sprinkle with oats. Place on cookie sheet. Bake about 8 minutes or until light golden brown. Remove from cookie sheet to wire rack; cool.

■ **1 Bagel:** 150 calories (0 calories from fat); 0g fat (0g saturated); 0mg cholesterol; 290mg sodium; 34g carbohydrate (1g dietary fiber); 4g protein

Berry Bagels: Add 1/2 cup dried blueberries, cherries or cranberries at the Raisin/Nut signal or 5 to 10 minutes before the last kneading cycle ends.

Cinnamon Bagels: Add 1 teaspoon ground cinnamon with the salt.

Garlic Bagels: Add 1 teaspoon garlic powder with the salt.

Parmesan Twists

10 twists

3/4 cup water

2 cups bread flour

1 teaspoon salt

1 tablespoon sugar

1 teaspoon bread machine or quick active dry yeast

1/3 cup margarine or butter, melted

2 tablespoons grated Parmesan cheese

Measure carefully, placing all ingredients except margarine and cheese in bread machine pan in the order recommended by the manufacturer.

Select Dough/Manual cycle. Do not use delay cycles.

Remove dough from pan, using lightly floured hands. Place dough in greased bowl, and turn greased side up. Cover and let rise in warm place about 30 minutes or until double. (Dough is ready if indentation remains when touched.)

Grease cookie sheet. Punch down dough. Divide dough into 20 equal pieces. Roll each piece into 10- to 12-inch rope on lightly floured surface. Pinch ends of 2 ropes together and twist ropes together, starting at pinched end. Place twists on cookie sheet; tuck other ends under. Mix margarine and cheese; brush over twists. Cover and let rise in warm place 20 to 30 minutes or until double.

Heat oven to 400°. Bake 12 to 15 minutes or until golden brown. Serve warm, or cool on wire rack.

■ 1 Twist: 165 calories (65 calories from fat); 7 fat (2g saturated); 0mg cholesterol; 300mg sodium; 23g carbohydrate (1g dietary fiber); 3g protein

SUCCESS TIP

Twist the ropes together gently so the dough doesn't stretch. The twist will have a nicer appearance after baking.

TRY THIS

Like a little crunch on your twists? Instead of adding Parmesan cheese to the melted margarine, brush the twists with just the melted margarine, then sprinkle with your favorite seed such as sesame, poppy or caraway.

SHAPING

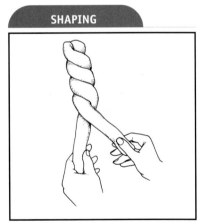

Pinch ends of 2 ropes together and twist ropes together, starting at pinched end.

Cheese-Filled Breadsticks

TRY THIS

Like a breadstick with a "string" attached? Use mozzarella cheese instead of Cheddar because mozzarella becomes stringy when melted. Swiss or Monterey Jack cheese would also make great-tasting breadsticks.

DO-AHEAD NOTE

After you have shaped and filled the dough on the cookie sheet, cover with plastic wrap. You can refrigerate the dough from 4 hours up to 48 hours. Before baking, remove the dough from the refrigerator and remove plastic wrap. Cover with kitchen towel and let rise in a warm place about 1 1/2 hours or until almost double. Bake as the recipe tells you.

SHAPING

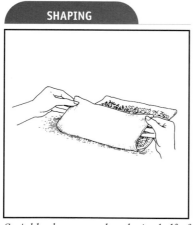

Sprinkle cheese over lengthwise half of rectangle. Fold dough lengthwise in half over cheese; pinch to seal edges.

15 breadsticks

2/3 cup water

1 tablespoon vegetable oil

2 cups bread flour

2 teaspoons chili powder

1 1/2 teaspoons sugar

3/4 teaspoon salt

1 1/4 teaspoons bread machine or quick active dry yeast

1 cup shredded Cheddar cheese (4 ounces)

Measure carefully, placing all ingredients except cheese in bread machine pan in the order recommended by the manufacturer.

Select Dough/Manual cycle. Do not use delay cycles.

Remove dough from pan, using lightly floured hands. Cover and let rest 10 minutes on lightly floured surface.

Grease large cookie sheet. Roll or pat dough into 15 × 9-inch rectangle; place on cookie sheet. Sprinkle cheese over lengthwise half of rectangle. Fold dough lengthwise in half over cheese; pinch to seal edges. Cover and let rise in warm place 15 to 20 minutes or until almost double.

Heat oven to 375°. Sprinkle with additional chili powder if desired. Bake 18 to 20 minutes or until golden brown. Remove from cookie sheet to wire rack. Cool at least 10 minutes. Cut crosswise into fifteen 1-inch breadsticks.

■ 1 Breadstick: 110 calories (35 calories from fat); 4g fat (2g saturated); 10mg cholesterol; 170mg sodium; 15g carbohydrate (1g dietary fiber); 4g protein

Hit-the-Trail Breadsticks

DO-AHEAD NOTE

After you have shaped the dough into ropes and placed them on the cookie sheet, cover with plastic wrap. You can refrigerate them from 4 hours up to 48 hours. Before baking, remove the breadsticks from the refrigerator and remove plastic wrap. Cover with kitchen towel and let rise in a warm place about 1 1/2 hours or until double. Bake the breadsticks as the recipe tells you.

DID YOU KNOW?

Trail mix is a mixture of seeds, nuts and dried fruits. Sometimes it will have added goodies, such as candy-covered chocolate candies, chocolate, butterscotch or peanut butter chips and even coconut or banana chips. Pick your favorite mix for these flavor-packed breadsticks.

12 breadsticks

1 cup plus 2 tablespoons water

2 tablespoons vegetable oil

3 1/4 cups bread flour

2/3 cup trail mix

1/4 cup packed brown sugar

1 teaspoon salt

1 1/2 teaspoons bread machine or quick active dry yeast

Measure carefully, placing all ingredients in bread machine pan in the order recommended by the manufacturer.

Select Dough/Manual cycle. Do not use delay cycles.

Remove dough from pan, using lightly floured hands. Cover and let rest 10 minutes on lightly floured surface.

Grease large cookie sheet. Divide dough into 12 equal pieces. Roll each piece into 7-inch rope. Place 1 inch apart on cookie sheet. Brush with additional vegetable oil. Cover and let rise in warm place 5 to 15 minutes or until almost double.

Heat oven to 375°. Bake 15 to 20 minutes or until golden brown. Serve warm, or cool on wire rack.

■ 1 Breadstick: 200 calories (45 calories from fat); 5g fat (1g saturated); 0mg cholesterol; 220mg sodium; 36g carbohydrate (2g dietary fiber); 5g protein

Dried Cherry Petits Pains

12 petits pains

3/4 cup milk

1/4 cup margarine or butter, softened

2 eggs

3 1/3 cups bread flour

3 tablespoons sugar

1 teaspoon salt

1/2 teaspoon ground mace

1 teaspoon finely shredded orange peel

2 teaspoons bread machine or quick active dry yeast

1/2 cup dried cherries

1 egg white

1 tablespoon water

Measure carefully, placing all ingredients except dried cherries, egg white and water in bread machine pan in the order recommended by the manufacturer. Add cherries at the Raisin/Nut signal.

Select Dough/Manual cycle. Do not use delay cycles.

Remove dough from pan, using lightly floured hands. Cover and let rest 10 minutes on lightly floured surface.

Grease large cookie sheet. Divide dough into 12 equal pieces; shape each piece into a smooth ball. Place about 2 inches apart on cookie sheet. Cover and let rise in warm place 20 to 30 minutes or until almost double.

Heat oven to 375°. Make 3 parallel slashes, about 1/4 inch deep, in top of each roll, using sharp knife. Lightly beat egg white and water; brush over tops of rolls. Bake 15 to 18 minutes or until dark golden brown. Remove from cookie sheet to wire rack; cool.

■ 1 Petit Pain: 215 calories (45 calories from fat); 5g fat (1g saturated); 35mg cholesterol; 270mg sodium; 39g carbohydrate (3g dietary fiber); 6g protein

SUCCESS TIP

If your bread machine doesn't have a Raisin/Nut signal, add the cherries 5 to 10 minutes before the last kneading cycle ends. Check your bread machine's use-and-care book to find out how long the last cycle runs.

DO-AHEAD NOTE

After you have shaped the dough into rolls and placed them on the cookie sheet, cover with plastic wrap. You can refrigerate them from 4 hours up to 48 hours. Before baking, remove the rolls from the refrigerator and remove plastic wrap. Cover with kitchen towel and let rise in a warm place about 1 1/2 hours or until double. Then cut and brush the tops and bake as the recipe tells you.

TRY THIS

For a fall breakfast treat, use dried cranberries instead of the cherries. Or you may want to try raisins instead of the cherries and cinnamon instead of the mace for a family favorite.

Crusty Homemade Bread Bowls

SUCCESS TIP

When placing the dough circle over the cup, don't let the dough curl under the edge of the cup. It will bake onto the edge of the cup and be difficult to remove. If some of the dough should bake onto the edge, use the point of a paring knife to carefully separate it from the cup.

TRY THIS

These bread bowls are not only fun to use but are also great to eat. Fill the bowl with a crisp green salad and serve as a side dish. Or fill it with a thick, chunky stew or your favorite main-dish salad.

6 bread bowls

1 cup water

2 3/4 cups bread flour

1 tablespoon sugar

1 teaspoon salt

1 1/2 teaspoons bread machine or quick active dry yeast

1 egg yolk

1 tablespoon water

Measure carefully, placing all ingredients except egg yolk and 1 tablespoon water in bread machine pan in the order recommended by the manufacturer.

Select Dough/Manual cycle. Do not use delay cycles.

Remove dough from pan, using lightly floured hands. Cover and let rest 10 minutes on lightly floured surface.

Grease outsides of six 10-ounce custard cups. Place cups upside down on ungreased cookie sheet. Divide dough into 6 equal pieces. Roll or pat each piece into 7-inch circle on lightly floured surface. Shape dough circles over outsides of cups. Cover and let rise in warm place 15 to 20 minutes or until slightly puffy.

Heat oven to 375°. Mix egg yolk and 1 tablespoon water; brush gently over bread bowls. Bake 18 to 22 minutes or until golden brown. Carefully lift bread bowls from custard cups—bread and cups will be hot. Cool bread bowls upright on wire rack.

■ 1 Bread Bowl: 204 calories (20 calories from fat); 2g fat (0g saturated); 35mg cholesterol; 360mg sodium; 50g carbohydrate (2g dietary fiber); 7g protein

Crusty Homemade Bread Bowls

Dried Blueberry Lemon Rolls

SUCCESS TIP

If your bread machine doesn't have a Raisin/Nut signal, add the blueberries 5 to 10 minutes before the last kneading cycle ends. Check your bread machine's use-and-care book for how long the last cycle runs.

SUCCESS TIP

Use a sharp knife with a straight edge to slash the tops of the rolls. If the knife blade is dull, it may tear the dough rather than cut it. This could cause the dough to lose some volume and might be a little smaller after rolls are baked.

DO-AHEAD NOTE

Shape into rolls and place on the cookie sheet; cover with plastic wrap. Refrigerate from 4 hours up to 48 hours. Before baking, remove plastic wrap. Cover with kitchen towel and let rise in a warm place about 2 hours or until double. Then cut and brush the tops and bake.

12 rolls

3/4 cup milk

1/4 cup margarine or butter, softened

2 eggs

3 1/3 cups bread flour

3 tablespoons sugar

1 teaspoon salt

1/2 teaspoon ground nutmeg

1 teaspoon finely shredded lemon peel

2 teaspoons bread machine or quick active dry yeast

1/2 cup dried blueberries

1 egg white

1 tablespoon water

Lemon Glaze (below)

Measure all ingredients except dried blueberries, egg white, water and Lemon Glaze in bread machine pan in the order recommended by the manufacturer. Add blueberries at the Raisin/Nut signal.

Select Dough/Manual cycle. Do not use delay cycles. Remove dough from pan, using lightly floured hands. Cover and let rest 10 minutes on lightly floured surface.

Grease large cookie sheet. Divide dough into 12 equal pieces; shape each piece into a smooth ball. Place about 2 inches apart on cookie sheet. Cover and let rise in warm place 20 to 30 minutes or until almost double.

Heat oven to 375°. Make 1 lengthwise slash, about 1/4 inch deep, in top of each roll, using sharp knife. Lightly beat egg white and water; brush over tops of rolls. Bake 15 to 18 minutes or until dark golden brown. Remove from cookie sheet to wire rack; cool. Drizzle with Lemon Glaze. Serve warm, or let cool on wire rack.

Lemon Glaze

1/2 cup powdered sugar

2 to 3 teaspoons lemon juice

Mix ingredients until smooth and thin enough to drizzle.

■ 1 Roll: 250 calories (65 calories from fat); 6g fat (3g saturated); 45mg cholesterol; 150mg sodium; 44g carbohydrate (3g dietary fiber); 6g protein

Strawberry and Poppy Seed Rolls

15 rolls

1/2 cup water

4 drops red food color, if desired

3/4 cup frozen strawberries (without syrup), thawed and drained

2 tablespoons margarine or butter, softened

3 1/4 cups bread flour

2 teaspoons poppy seed

1/4 cup sugar

1 1/4 teaspoons salt

1 3/4 teaspoons bread machine or quick active dry yeast

1 egg, slightly beaten, if desired

White baking chips or semisweet chocolate chips, melted, if desired

Measure carefully, placing all ingredients except egg and baking chips in bread machine pan in the order recommended by the manufacturer.

Select Dough/Manual cycle. Do not use delay cycles.

Remove dough from pan, using lightly floured hands. Cover and let rest 15 minutes on lightly floured surface.

Grease large cookie sheet. Divide dough into 15 equal pieces. Shape each piece into a ball. Place 2 inches apart on cookie sheet. Cover and let rise 30 to 40 minutes or until double. (Dough is ready if indentation remains when touched.)

Heat oven to 375°. Brush tops of rolls with egg. Bake 12 to 15 minutes or until golden brown. Remove from cookie sheet to wire rack. Cool completely. Drizzle melted baking chips over tops of rolls, or dip tops of rolls into melted baking chips.

■ 1 Roll: 135 calories (20 calories from fat); 2g fat (0g saturated); 0mg cholesterol; 210mg sodium; 27g carbohydrate (1g dietary fiber); 3g protein

SUCCESS TIP

If you melt the baking chips in the microwave, be careful not to overheat them. Chips don't melt and lose their shape in the microwave like they do when you melt them on the stove. Instead, they hold their shape and become shiny when they are hot. Give your chips a stir several times while you microwave them and you'll see them melting pefectly.

DO-AHEAD NOTE

After you have shaped the dough into rolls and placed them on the cookie sheet, cover with plastic wrap. You can refrigerate them from 4 hours up to 48 hours. Before baking, remove the rolls from the refrigerator and remove plastic wrap. Cover with kitchen towel and let rise in a warm place about 2 hours or until double. Then brush the tops and bake as the recipe tells you.

Orange Pecan Buns

DO-AHEAD NOTE

After you have shaped the dough into buns and placed them on the cookie sheet, cover with plastic wrap. You can refrigerate them from 4 hours up to 48 hours. Before baking, remove the buns from the refrigerator and remove plastic wrap. Cover with kitchen towel and let rise in a warm place about 2 hours or until double. Then brush the buns and bake as the recipe tells you.

SHAPING

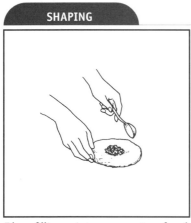

Place filling mixture on center of each circle.

Bring edges of dough up over filling; pinch edges to seal.

12 buns

1 cup milk

1/4 cup sour cream

1 tablespoon orange marmalade

3 cups bread flour

1 tablespoon sugar

1 teaspoon salt

2 teaspoons bread machine or quick active dry yeast

1/2 cup orange marmalade

1/3 cup chopped pecans, toasted (see Note)

1 egg, beaten

Vanilla Glaze (page 223), if desired

Measure carefully, placing all ingredients except 1/2 cup marmalade, the pecans, egg and Vanilla Glaze in bread machine pan in the order recommended by the manufacturer.

Select Dough/Manual cycle. Do not use delay cycles.

Remove dough from pan, using lightly floured hands. Cover and let rest 10 minutes on lightly floured surface.

Grease large cookie sheet. Mix 1/2 cup marmalade and the pecans; set aside. Divide dough into 12 equal pieces. Flatten each piece into 3 1/2-inch circle. Place 1 rounded teaspoon marmalade mixture on center of each circle. Bring edges of dough up over filling; pinch edges to seal. Place buns, pinched sides down and about 2 inches apart, on cookie sheet. Cover and let rise in warm place 30 to 45 minutes or until double. (Dough is ready if indentation remains when touched.)

Heat oven to 350°. Brush egg over buns. Bake 15 to 20 minutes or until golden brown. Drizzle Vanilla Glaze over warm rolls. Serve warm.

■ 1 Bun: 185 calories (35 calories from fat); 4g fat (1g saturated); 20mg cholesterol; 220mg sodium; 33g carbohydrate (1g dietary fiber); 5g protein

NOTE: Toast pecans in a 350° oven in an uncovered shallow pan, stirring them occasionally so they toast evenly. The toasting will take about 10 minutes, and you will smell the wonderful aroma of pecans. When they are toasted, remove from the pan so they won't overtoast.

Pear Kuchen with Ginger Topping (page 215) and Orange Pecan Buns

Festive Raspberry Rolls

SHAPING

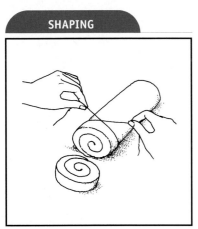

Cut roll into equal slices.

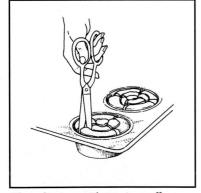

Place slices, cut side up, in muffin cups. Snip through each slice twice, cutting into fourths, using kitchen scissors.

12 rolls

1/3 cup milk

1/3 cup water

3 tablespoons margarine or butter, softened

1 egg

2 cups bread flour

1/3 cup sugar

1/2 teaspoon salt

1 3/4 teaspoons bread machine or quick active dry yeast

3 tablespoons raspberry preserves

Measure carefully, placing all ingredients except preserves in bread machine pan in the order recommended by the manufacturer.

Select Dough/Manual cycle. Do not use delay cycles.

Remove dough from pan, using lightly floured hands. Cover and let rest 10 minutes on lightly floured surface.

Grease 12 medium muffin cups, 2 1/2 × 1 1/4 inches. Roll or pat dough into 15 × 10-inch rectangle. Spread preserves over dough to within 1/4 inch of edges. Roll up dough, beginning at 15-inch side; pinch edge of dough into roll to seal. Stretch and shape roll to make even.

Cut roll into 12 equal slices. Place slices, cut sides up, in muffin cups. Snip through each slice twice, cutting into fourths, using kitchen scissors. Gently spread dough pieces open. Cover and let rise in warm place about 25 minutes or until double. (Dough is ready if indentation remains when touched.)

Heat oven to 375°. Bake 15 to 20 minutes or until golden brown. Immediately remove from pan to wire rack. Serve warm, or cool on wire rack.

■ 1 Roll: 145 calories (35 calories from fat); 4g fat (1g saturated); 20mg cholesterol; 140mg sodium; 25g carbohydrate (1g dietary fiber); 3g protein

Hot Cross Buns

SUCCESS TIP

If your bread machine doesn't have a Raisin/Nut signal, add the raisins 5 to 10 minutes before the last kneading cycle ends. Check your bread machine's use-and-care book for how long the last cycle runs.

SUCCESS TIP

We like to use only butter to make these rich-tasting buns.

DO-AHEAD NOTE

After you have shaped the dough into buns and snipped the cross in top of each, cover with plastic wrap. You can refrigerate them from 4 hours up to 24 hours. Before baking, remove the buns from the refrigerator and remove plastic wrap. Cover with kitchen towel and let rise in a warm place about 2 hours or until double. Then brush the tops and bake as the recipe tells you.

16 buns

2 eggs plus enough water to equal 1 1/3 cups

1/2 cup butter, softened

4 cups bread flour

3/4 teaspoon ground cinnamon

1/4 teaspoon ground nutmeg

1 1/2 teaspoons salt

2 tablespoons sugar

1 1/2 teaspoons bread machine or quick active dry yeast

1/2 cup dark raisins

1/2 cup golden raisins

1 egg

2 tablespoons cold water

White Icing (below)

Measure carefully, placing all ingredients except raisins, 1 egg, the cold water and White Icing in bread machine pan in the order recommended by the manufacturer. Add raisins at the Raisin/Nut signal.

Select Dough/Manual cycle. Do not use delay cycles.

Remove dough from pan, using lightly floured hands. Cover and let rest 10 minutes on lightly floured surface.

Grease cookie sheet or 2 round pans, 9 × 1 1/2 inches. Divide dough in half. Divide each half into 8 equal pieces. Shape each piece into a smooth ball. Place about 2 inches apart on cookie sheet or 1 inch apart in pans. Snip a cross shape in top of each ball, using scissors. Cover and let rise in warm place about 40 minutes or until double.

Heat oven to 375°. Beat egg and cold water slightly; brush on buns. Bake 18 to 20 minutes or until golden brown. Remove from cookie sheet to rack. Cool slightly. Make a cross on bun with White Icing.

White Icing

1 cup powdered sugar

1 tablespoon milk or water

1/2 teaspoon vanilla

Mix all ingredients until smooth and spreadable.

■ 1 Bun: 245 calories (65 calories from fat); 7g fat (4g saturated); 30mg cholesterol; 240mg sodium; 43g carbohydrate (1g dietary fiber); 4g protein

Hot Cross Buns

COMPLIMENTS
of
Betty's B&B

Chocolate S'mores Buns

SUCCESS TIP

When you bring the dough up over the marshmallow, be careful not to stretch the dough too thin or to make holes in the dough, or the filling will bubble out during baking. Not only will you lose the great chocolate and marshmallow filling, but the muffin pan will be a mess to clean.

SUCCESS TIP

We found that miniature chocolate chips work best in these buns. They were easy to mix with the graham cracker crumbs.

SHAPING

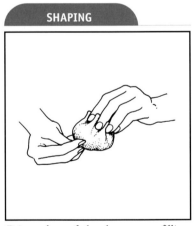

Bring edges of dough up over filling; pinch edges to seal.

12 buns

1 cup water

2 tablespoons margarine or butter, softened

2 3/4 cups bread flour

2/3 cup miniature semisweet chocolate chips

1/4 cup sugar

1 teaspoon salt

2 1/4 teaspoons bread machine or quick active dry yeast

S'mores Filling (below)

12 large marshmallows

1/4 cup miniature semisweet chocolate chips or white baking chips, melted, if desired

Measure carefully, placing all ingredients except S'mores Filling, marshmallows and 1/4 cup melted chocolate chips in bread machine pan in the order recommended by the manufacturer.

Select Dough/Manual cycle. Do not use delay cycles.

Remove dough from pan, using lightly floured hands. Cover and let rest 10 minutes on lightly floured surface. Prepare S'mores Filling.

Grease 12 medium muffin cups, 2 1/2 × 1 1/4 inches. Divide dough into 12 equal pieces. Pat each piece into 3 1/2-inch circle. Place 1 tablespoon filling and 1 marshmallow on center of each circle. Bring edges of dough up over marshmallow; pinch edges to seal. Place pinched sides down in muffin cups. Cover and let rise in warm place 35 to 40 minutes or until almost double.

Heat oven to 375°. Bake 20 to 25 minutes or until buns sound hollow when tapped. Remove from pan to wire rack. Cool completely. Drizzle with melted chocolate chips.

S'mores Filling

1/3 cup miniature semisweet chocolate chips

1/3 cup graham cracker crumbs

2 tablespoons margarine or butter, melted

Mix all ingredients.

■ 1 Bun: 260 calories (80 calories from fat); 9g fat (4g saturated); 0mg cholesterol; 260mg sodium; 43g carbohydrate (2g dietary fiber); 4g protein

Sugared Doughnuts

20 doughnuts

2/3 cup milk

1/4 cup water

1/4 cup margarine or butter, softened

1 egg

3 cups bread flour

1/4 cup sugar

1 teaspoon salt

2 1/2 teaspoons bread machine or quick active dry yeast

Vegetable oil

Additional sugar, if desired

Measure carefully, placing all ingredients except vegetable oil and additional sugar in bread machine pan in the order recommended by the manufacturer.

Select Dough/Manual cycle. Do not use delay cycles.

Remove dough from pan, using lightly floured hands. Cover and let rest 10 minutes on lightly floured board.

Roll dough 3/8 inch thick on lightly floured board. Cut with floured doughnut cutter. Cover and let rise on board 35 to 45 minutes or until slightly raised.

Heat 2 to 3 inches oil in deep fryer or heavy Dutch oven to 375°. Fry 2 or 3 doughnuts at a time 2 to 3 minutes, turning as they rise to the surface, until golden brown. Remove from oil with long fork or slotted spoon. Drain on wire rack. Roll warm doughnuts in sugar.

■ 1 Doughnut: 185 calories (100 calories from fat); 11g fat (2g saturated); 10mg cholesterol; 140mg sodium; 19g carbohydrate (1g dietary fiber); 3g protein

SUCCESS TIP

Use a deep-fat frying thermometer to be sure the oil temperature is correct. If the oil is too hot, the doughnuts will be golden brown but will not be cooked inside. If the oil is not hot enough, the doughnuts will absorb too much oil and be greasy.

TRY THIS

If you don't have a doughnut cutter, you still can make great doughnuts. Roll the dough out into a rectangle until it is 3/8 inch thick. Cut the dough into 20 squares. With your fingers, form a hole about an inch wide in the center of each square. The hole will help the doughnut fry evenly, so the center will not be undercooked and doughy. Try covering these square doughnuts with powdered sugar and a touch of cinnamon. Yum!

Honey Lemon Sweet Rolls

SUCCESS TIP

After rolling the dough, be sure to pinch the edge of the dough into the roll so it is sealed. This will help the slices keep their shape when you cut them and keep the end from popping out

SUCCESS TIP

A quick and easy way to cut the slices from the roll is to use dental floss. The floss makes a clean cut and doesn't cause the slice or end of the roll to flatten. To cut, place a length of dental floss under the roll where you want to cut a slice. Bring the ends of the floss up and criss-cross them at top of roll. Pull ends in opposite directions, and the floss will cut a nice, even slice.

DO-AHEAD NOTE

After you have placed the slices in the pan, cover with plastic wrap. You can refrigerate them from 4 hours up to 48 hours. Before baking, remove the rolls from the refrigerator and remove plastic wrap. Cover with kitchen towel and let rise in a warm place about 2 hours or until double. Bake the rolls as the recipe tells you.

9 rolls

3/4 cup plus 2 tablespoons water

2 tablespoons margarine or butter, softened

2 1/2 cups bread flour

1/4 cup sugar

1 teaspoon salt

1 teaspoon bread machine or quick active dry yeast

Honey Lemon Filling (right)

1 tablespoon margarine or butter, softened

Honey Glaze (right)

Measure carefully, placing all ingredients except Honey Lemon Filling, 1 tablespoon margarine and Honey Glaze in bread machine pan in the order recommended by the manufacturer.

Select Dough/Manual cycle. Do not use delay cycles.

Remove dough from pan, using lightly floured hands. Cover and let rest 10 minutes on lightly floured surface. Prepare Honey Lemon Filling.

Grease square pan, $9 \times 9 \times 2$ inches. Flatten dough with hands or rolling pin into 9-inch square. Spread 1 tablespoon margarine over dough. Spoon filling by scant teaspoonfuls evenly over dough. Roll dough up tightly; pinch edge of dough into roll to seal. Stretch and shape roll to make even. Cut into nine 1-inch slices. Place in pan. Cover and let rise in warm place 1 to 1 1/4 hours or until double. (Dough is ready if indentation remains when touched.)

Heat oven to 375°. Bake 25 to 30 minutes or until golden brown. Remove from pan to wire rack. Drizzle Honey Glaze over warm rolls. Serve warm.

Honey Lemon Filling

1/3 cup chopped pecans

1/3 cup golden raisins

1 tablespoon sugar

3 tablespoons honey

1/2 teaspoon grated lemon peel

3/4 teaspoon lemon juice

Mix all ingredients.

Honey Glaze

1/4 cup sugar

1/4 cup honey

1 tablespoon margarine or butter

1 1/2 teaspoons grated lemon peel

Heat all ingredients to boiling over medium-high heat; reduce heat. Simmer uncovered about 3 minutes or until thickened.

■ 1 Roll: 330 calories (70 calories from fat); 8g fat (1g saturated); 0mg cholesterol; 300mg sodium; 61g carbohydrate (2g dietary fiber); 5g protein

TRY THIS

For added color and a different flavor twist, use dried blueberries or cherries instead of the golden raisins in the filling.

SHAPING

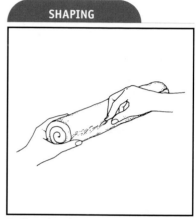

Roll up dough; pinch edge of dough into roll to seal.

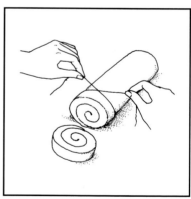

Cut roll into equal slices.

Glazed Cinnamon Rolls

DO-AHEAD NOTE

After you have placed the slices in the pan, cover with plastic wrap. You can refrigerate them from 4 hours up to 48 hours. Before baking, remove the rolls from the refrigerator and remove plastic wrap. Cover and kitchen towel and let rise in a warm place about 2 hours or until double. Bake the rolls as the recipe tells you.

TRY THIS

Have a jar of pumpkin pie spice or apple pie spice in your cupboard? Take a break from the traditional cinnamon and "spice up" these rolls by substituting one of these blends for a little flavor twist.

15 rolls

1 egg plus enough water to equal 1 cup plus 1 tablespoon

1/4 cup margarine or butter, softened

3 1/2 cups bread flour

1 teaspoon salt

1/3 cup sugar

1 1/2 teaspoons bread machine or quick active dry yeast

Cinnamon Walnut Filling (below)

2 tablespoons margarine or butter, softened

Vanilla Glaze (page 223)

Measure carefully, placing all ingredients except Cinnamon Walnut Filling, 2 tablespoons margarine and Vanilla Glaze in bread machine pan in the order recommended by the manufacturer.

Select Dough/Manual cycle. Do not use delay cycles.

Remove dough from pan. Cover and let rest 10 minutes on lightly floured surface. Prepare Cinnamon Walnut Filling.

Grease rectangular pan, 13 × 9 × 2 inches. Flatten dough with hands or rolling pin into 15 × 9-inch rectangle. Spread 2 tablespoons margarine over dough; sprinkle with filling. Roll up tightly, beginning at 15-inch side; pinch edge of dough into roll to seal (see Shaping, page 196). Stretch and shape roll to make even. Cut into fifteen 1-inch slices. Place slightly apart in pan. Cover and let rise in warm place about 40 minutes or until double. (Dough is ready if indentation remains when touched.)

Heat oven to 375°. Bake 23 to 28 minutes or until golden brown. Remove from pan to wire rack. Drizzle Vanilla Glaze over warm rolls.

Cinnamon Walnut Filling

1/3 cup packed brown sugar

1/4 cup finely chopped walnuts

1/4 cup raisins

2 teaspoons ground cinnamon

Mix all ingredients.

■ 1 Roll: 245 calories (65 calories from fat); 7g fat (1g saturated); 15mg cholesterol; 200mg sodium; 42g carbohydrate (1g dietary fiber); 4g protein

Sticky Rolls

15 rolls

1 cup water

1 egg

1/4 cup margarine or butter, softened

3 1/2 cups bread flour

1 teaspoon salt

1/3 cup sugar

1 1/2 teaspoons bread machine or quick active dry yeast

Caramel Topping (below)

2 tablespoons margarine or butter, softened

Cinnamon Filling (below)

Measure carefully, placing all ingredients except Caramel Topping, 2 tablespoons margarine and Cinnamon Filling in bread machine pan in the order recommended by the manufacturer.

Select Dough/Manual cycle. Do not use delay cycles.

Remove dough from pan, using lightly floured hands. Cover and let rest 10 minutes on lightly floured surface. Prepare Caramel Topping.

Roll or pat dough into 15 × 10-inch rectangle on lightly floured surface. Spread 2 tablespoons margarine over dough. Prepare Cinnamon Filling; sprinkle over margarine. Roll dough up tightly, beginning at 15-inch side; pinch edge of dough into roll to seal. Stretch and shape roll to make even. Cut roll into fifteen 1-inch slices. Place slightly apart in pan. Cover and let rise in warm place about 1 hour or until double.

Heat oven to 350°. Bake 35 to 40 minutes or until golden brown. Immediately turn pan upside down onto heatproof serving platter or tray. Let pan remain over rolls 1 minute; remove pan. Serve rolls warm.

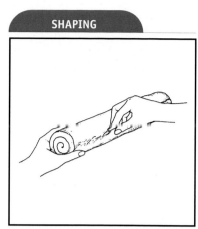

Roll up dough; pinch edge of dough into roll to seal.

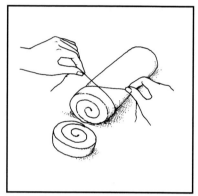

Cut roll into equal slices.

Caramel Topping

Place 1/2 cup melted margarine or butter in ungreased rectangular pan, 13×9×2 inches. Stir in 1 cup packed brown sugar and 1/4 cup corn syrup until well blended. Spread evenly in pan.

Cinnamon Filling

Mix 2 tablespoons packed brown sugar, 2 tablespoons granulated sugar and 1 teaspoon ground cinnamon together.

■ 1 Roll: 315 calories (100 calories from fat); 11g fat (2g saturated); 15mg cholesterol; 290mg sodium; 51g carbohydrate (1g dietary fiber); 4g protein

Chocolate Caramel Sticky Buns

DO-AHEAD NOTE

Cover the slices in the pan. Refrigerate them from 4 hours up to 48 hours. Before baking, remove the plastic wrap, cover with kitchen towel and let rise in a warm place 2 hours or until double. Bake the buns.

SHAPING

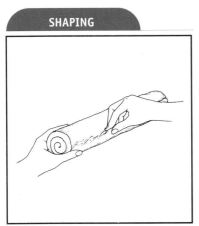

Roll up dough; pinch edge of dough into roll to seal.

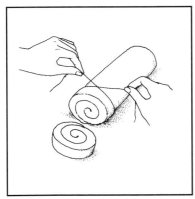

Cut roll into equal slices.

15 buns

3/4 cup water

1/3 cup margarine or butter, softened

1 egg

3 cups bread flour

1/2 cup baking cocoa

1/3 cup granulated sugar

1/2 teaspoon salt

3 teaspoons bread machine or quick active dry yeast

Caramel Topping (page 205)

3/4 cup pecan halves

2 tablespoons margarine or butter, softened

Chocolate Chip Filling (below)

Measure carefully, placing all ingredients except Caramel Topping, pecans, 2 tablespoons margarine and Chocolate Chip Filling in bread machine pan in the order recommended by the manufacturer.

Select Dough/Manual cycle. Do not use delay cycles.

Remove dough from pan. Cover and let rest 10 minutes on lightly floured surface. Prepare Caramel Topping in ungreased rectangular pan, 13 × 9 × 2 inches. Sprinkle with pecans.

Roll dough into 15 × 10-inch rectangle on lightly floured surface. Spread 2 tablespoons margarine over dough. Prepare Chocolate Chip Filling; sprinkle over margarine. Roll dough up tightly, beginning at 15-inch side; pinch edge of dough into roll to seal. Stretch and shape roll to make even. Cut roll into fifteen 1-inch slices. Place slightly apart in pan. Cover and let rise in warm place about 30 minutes or until double.

Heat oven to 350°. Bake 30 to 35 minutes or until dark brown. Immediately turn pan upside down onto heatproof serving platter or tray. Let pan remain over buns 1 minute; remove pan.

Chocolate Chip Filling

Mix 1/2 cup miniature semisweet chocolate chips, 2 tablespoons packed brown sugar and 1 teaspoon ground cinnamon.

■ 1 Bun: 370 calories (160 calories from fat); 18g fat (4g saturated); 15mg cholesterol; 250mg sodium; 50g carbohydrate (3g dietary fiber); 5g protein

Chocolate Caramel Sticky Buns

Maple Walnut Twists

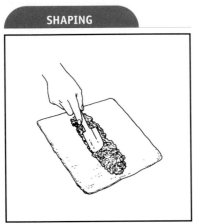

Spread filling lengthwise down center third of rectangle.

Fold one outer third of dough over filling; spread with remaining filling over folded dough.

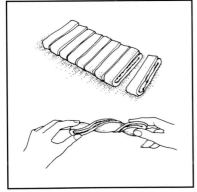

Cut crosswise into 16 1-inch strips. Holding a strip at each end, twist in opposite directions.

16 twists

1 cup water

1/4 cup margarine or butter, softened

1 egg

3 1/2 cups bread flour

1/3 cup sugar

1 teaspoon salt

1 1/2 teaspoons bread machine or quick active dry yeast

Walnut Filling (right)

Maple Icing (right)

Measure carefully, placing all ingredients except Walnut Filling and Maple Icing in bread machine pan in the order recommended by the manufacturer.

Select Dough/Manual cycle. Do not use delay cycles.

Remove dough from pan, using lightly floured hands. Cover and let rest 10 minutes on lightly floured surface. Prepare Walnut Filling.

Grease rectangular pan, 13 × 9 × 2 inches. Roll or pat dough into 16 × 10-inch rectangle on lightly floured surface. Spread half of the filling lengthwise down center third of rectangle. Fold one outer third of dough over filling; spread remaining filling over folded dough. Fold remaining third of dough over filling; pinch edge to seal.

Cut crosswise into sixteen 1-inch strips. Holding a strip at each end, twist in opposite directions. Place strips about 1 inch apart in pan, forming 2 rows of 8 strips each. Cover and let rise in warm place 50 to 60 minutes or until double. (Dough is ready if indentation remains when touched.)

Heat oven to 350°. Bake 35 to 40 minutes or until golden brown. Drizzle Maple Icing over warm twists. Serve warm.

Maple Walnut Twists

Walnut Filling

1/4 cup finely chopped walnuts

2 tablespoons maple-flavored syrup

2 tablespoons margarine or butter, softened

1/2 teaspoon ground cinnamon

Mix all ingredients.

Maple Icing

1 cup powdered sugar

1/2 teaspoon maple extract

About 1 tablespoon milk

Mix all ingredients until smooth and thin enough to drizzle.

■ 1 Twist: 190 calories (55 calories from fat); 6g fat (1g saturated); 15mg cholesterol; 230mg sodium; 32g carbohydrate (1g dietary fiber); 3g protein

DO-AHEAD NOTE

After you have placed the twists in the pan, cover with plastic wrap. You can refrigerate them from 4 hours up to 48 hours. Before baking, remove the twists from the refrigerator and remove plastic wrap. Cover with kitchen towel and let rise in a warm place about 2 hours or until double. Bake the twists as the recipe tells you above.

Chapter Seven

Sweet Breads and Coffee Cakes

Honey Walnut Coffee Cake (page 220)

Easy Apple Coffee Cake

SHAPING

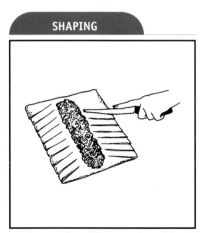

Make cuts from filling to edge of dough at 1-inch intervals.

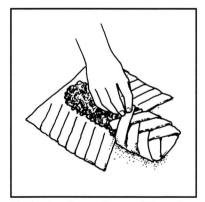

Fold strips diagonally over filling, alternating sides and overlapping in center.

1 coffee cake, 10 slices

2/3 cup water

3 tablespoons margarine or butter, softened

2 cups bread machine flour

3 tablespoons granulated sugar

1 teaspoon salt

1 1/2 teaspoons bread machine or quick active dry yeast

1 cup canned apple pie filling

Powdered sugar, if desired

Measure carefully, placing all ingredients except pie filling and powdered sugar in bread machine pan in the order recommended by the manufacturer.

Select Dough/Manual cycle. Do not use delay cycles.

Remove dough from pan, using lightly floured hands. Cover and let rest 10 minutes on lightly floured surface.

Grease large cookie sheet. Roll dough into 13 × 8-inch rectangle on lightly floured surface. Place on cookie sheet. Spoon pie filling lengthwise down center third of rectangle. On each 13-inch side, make cuts from filling to edge of dough at 1-inch intervals, using sharp knife. Fold ends up over filling. Fold strips diagonally over filling, alternating sides and overlapping in center. Cover and let rise in warm place 30 to 45 minutes or until double. (Dough is ready if indentation remains when touched.)

Heat oven to 375°. Bake 30 to 35 minutes or until golden brown. Remove from cookie sheet to wire rack; cool. Sprinkle with powdered sugar.

■ 1 Slice: 160 calories (35 calories from fat); 4g fat (1g saturated); 0mg cholesterol; 280mg sodium; 29g carbohydrate (1g dietary fiber); 3g protein

Pear Prune Braid

2 braids, 12 slices each

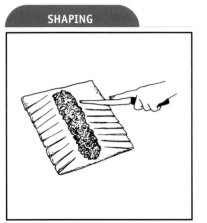

Make cuts from filling to edge of dough at 1-inch intervals.

Fold strips diagonally over filling, alternating sides and overlapping in center.

Pear-Prune Filling

Mix together 2 cups peeled and diced pears, 1 cup cut-up ready-to-eat pitted prunes, 1/4 cup chopped walnuts (if desired), 1/4 cup packed brown sugar, and 1 teaspoon ground cinnamon.

1/4 cup water

2 tablespoons margarine or butter, softened

1 cup sour cream

1 egg

3 cups bread flour or wheat blend bread flour

2 teaspoons bread machine or active dry

3 tablespoons packed brown sugar

1 teaspoon salt

Pear Prune Filling (below)

1 egg white

1 tablespoon water

White coarse sugar crystals (decorating sugar)

Measure carefully, placing all ingredients except Pear Prune Filling, egg white, 1 tablespoon water and sugar crystals in bread machine pan in the order recommended by the manufacturer.

Select Dough/Manual cycle. Do not use delay cycles.

Remove dough from pan, using lightly floured hands. Cover and let rest 10 minutes on lightly floured surface. Prepare Pear Prune Filling.

Grease 2 cookie sheets. Divide dough in half. Roll each half into 12 × 9-inch rectangle on lightly floured surface. Transfer each rectangle to cookie sheet. Spoon half of the filling lengthwise down center third of each rectangle. On each 12-inch side of each rectangle, make cuts from filling to edge of dough at 1-inch intervals, using sharp knife. Fold ends up over filling. Fold strips diagonally over filling, alternating sides and overlapping in center. Cover and let rise in warm 30 to 40 minutes or until double. (Dough is ready if indentation remains when touched.)

Heat oven to 375°. Lightly beat egg white and 1 tablespoon water; brush over tops of braids. Sprinkle with desired amount of sugar crystals. Bake 15 to 20 minutes or until golden brown. Remove from cookie sheet to wire rack; cool.

■ 1 Slice: 265 calories (65 calories from fat); 7g fat (3g saturated); 30mg cholesterol; 240mg sodium; 48g carbohydrate (3g dietary fiber); 6g protein

Pear Kuchen with Ginger Topping

1 coffee cake, 12 servings

1/2 cup milk

2 tablespoons margarine or butter, softened

1 egg

2 cups bread flour

2 tablespoons sugar

1 teaspoon salt

1 3/4 teaspoons bread machine or quick active dry yeast

Ginger Topping (below)

3 cups sliced fresh pears

1/2 cup whipping (heavy) cream

1 egg yolk

Measure carefully, placing all ingredients except Ginger Topping, pears, whipping cream and egg yolk in bread machine pan in the order recommended by the manufacturer.

Select Dough/Manual cycle. Do not use delay cycles.

Remove dough from pan, using lightly floured hands. Cover and let rest 10 minutes on lightly floured surface. Prepare Ginger Topping.

Grease rectangular pan, 13 × 9 × 2 inches. Press dough evenly in bottom of pan. Arrange pears on dough. Reserve 2 tablespoons of the topping; sprinkle remaining topping over pears. Cover and let rise in warm place 30 to 45 minutes or until double. (Dough is ready if indentation remains when touched.)

Heat oven to 375°. Bake 20 minutes. Mix whipping cream and egg yolk; pour over hot kuchen. Bake 15 minutes or until golden brown. Sprinkle with reserved 2 tablespoons topping. Serve warm.

Ginger Topping

1 cup sugar

2 tablespoons margarine or butter, softened

1 tablespoon chopped crystallized ginger

1 teaspoon ground cinnamon

Mix all ingredients.

■ 1 Serving: 230 calories (70 calories from fat); 8g fat (3g saturated); 45mg cholesterol; 260mg sodium; 38g carbohydrate (2g dietary fiber); 3g protein

SUCCESS TIP

Pears are flavorful and juicy when at their seasonal peak. If pears are not in season, you can make this kuchen with canned pears. You will need 3 cups of well-drained, canned sliced pears.

TRY THIS

When peaches are in season, make this custard-based kuchen with sliced fresh peaches. To peel the peaches easily, drop them into boiling water for just a minute, then remove them with a large slotted spoon. Immediately place them in iced water to stop the cooking. The peels will slip right off.

Cherry and White Chocolate Almond Twist

SUCCESS TIP

Be sure to use a sharp knife when cutting the roll lengthwise in half. This will help prevent the filling from pulling on the knife during cutting.

SHAPING

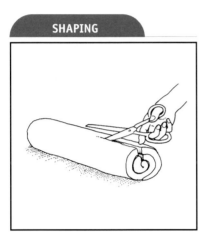

Cut roll lengthwise in half.

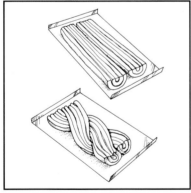

Place halves, filling side up and side by side, on cookie sheet; twist together gently and loosely.

1 twist, 16 slices

1/2 cup maraschino cherries

3/4 cup plus 2 tablespoons water

1 teaspoon almond extract

2 tablespoons margarine or butter

3 1/4 cups bread flour

2 tablespoons sugar

1 teaspoon salt

2 teaspoons bread machine or quick active dry yeast

White Chocolate Almond Topping (right)

2 tablespoons margarine or butter, softened

1/4 cup maraschino cherries, well drained

Cherry Glaze (right), if desired

Drain 1/2 cup cherries thoroughly; reserve 2 to 4 teaspoons cherry juice for Cherry Glaze.

Measure carefully, placing 1/2 cup cherries and remaining ingredients except White Chocolate Almond Topping, 2 tablespoons margarine, 1/4 cup cherries and Cherry Glaze in bread machine pan in the order recommended by the manufacturer.

Select Dough/Manual cycle. Do not use delay cycles.

Remove dough from pan, using lightly floured hands. Cover and let rest 10 minutes on lightly floured surface. Prepare White Chocolate Almond Topping.

Grease large cookie sheet. Roll dough into 15 × 10-inch rectangle. Spread 2 tablespoons margarine over dough. Sprinkle with topping and 1/4 cup cherries; press into dough. Roll up dough, beginning at 15-inch side. Place on cookie sheet.

Cut roll lengthwise in half. Place halves, filling sides up and side by side, on cookie sheet; twist together gently and loosely. Pinch ends to fasten. Cover and let rise in warm place about 45 minutes or until double.

Heat oven to 350°. Bake 30 to 35 minutes or until golden brown. Remove from sheet to wire rack. Cool. Drizzle with Cherry Glaze.

Cherry and White Chocolate Almond Twist

White Chocolate Almond Topping

1/2 cup chopped white baking chips

1/3 cup chopped slivered almonds

2 tablespoons sugar

Mix all ingredients.

Cherry Glaze

1/2 cup powdered sugar

2 to 4 teaspoons reserved maraschino cherry juice

Mix ingredients until smooth and thin enough to drizzle.

■ 1 Slice: 200 calories (55 calories from fat); 6g fat (2g saturated); 0mg cholesterol; 190mg sodium; 34g carbohydrate (1g dietary fiber); 4g protein

Apricot Cream Cheese Ring

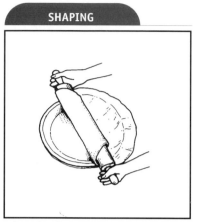

Place dough in pan, letting the side of dough hang over edge of pan.

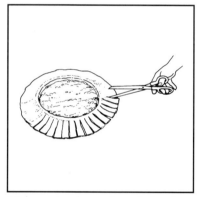

Make cuts along edge of dough at 1-inch intervals to about 1/2 inch above cream cheese mixture.

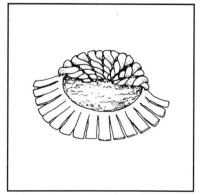

Twist pairs of strips of dough and fold over cream cheese mixture.

1 coffee cake, 10 servings

1/3 cup water

2 tablespoons margarine or butter, softened

1 egg

2 cups bread flour

2 tablespoons sugar

1/2 teaspoon salt

1 3/4 teaspoons bread machine or quick active dry yeast

1 package (3 ounces) cream cheese, softened

1 1/2 tablespoons bread flour

1/4 to 1/3 cup apricot preserves

1 egg, beaten, if desired

2 tablespoons sliced almonds

Measure carefully, placing all ingredients except cream cheese, 1 1/2 tablespoons flour, preserves, the beaten egg and almonds in bread machine pan in the order recommended by the manufacturer.

Select Dough/Manual cycle. Do not use delay cycles.

Remove dough from pan, using lightly floured hands. Cover and let rest 10 minutes on lightly floured surface. Mix cream cheese and 1 1/2 tablespoons flour.

Grease round pan, 9 × 1 1/2 inches. Roll dough into 15-inch circle. Place in pan, letting side of dough hang over edge of pan. Spread cream cheese mixture over dough in pan; spoon apricot preserves onto cream cheese mixture. Make cuts along edge of dough at 1-inch intervals to about 1/2 inch above cream cheese mixture. Twist pairs of dough strips and fold over cream cheese mixture. Cover and let rise in warm place 40 to 50 minutes or until almost double.

Heat oven to 375°. Brush beaten egg over dough. Sprinkle with almonds. Bake 30 to 35 minutes or until golden brown. Cool at least 30 minutes before cutting.

■ 1 Serving: 170 calories (65 calories from fat); 7g fat (3g saturated); 30mg cholesterol; 180mg sodium; 24g carbohydrate (1g dietary fiber); 4g protein

Apricot Cream Cheese Ring

Honey Walnut Coffee Cake

Spread filling crosswise over half of the rectangle; fold dough crosswise in half over filling; seal edges.

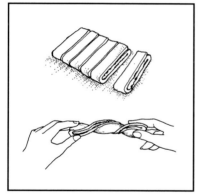

Cut rectangle crosswise into six 2-inch strips. Twist each strip loosely.

1 coffee cake, 12 servings

1/4 cup water

2/3 cup sour cream

2 tablespoons margarine or butter, softened

1 egg

3 cups bread flour

2 tablespoons granulated sugar

1 teaspoon salt

2 teaspoons bread machine or quick active dry yeast

Honey Walnut Filling (below)

1/4 cup margarine or butter, melted

1/3 cup packed brown sugar

1/4 cup honey

Measure carefully, placing all ingredients except Honey Walnut Filling, 1/4 cup margarine, the brown sugar and honey in bread machine pan in the order recommended by the manufacturer.

Select Dough/Manual cycle. Do not use delay cycles.

Remove dough from pan, using lightly floured hands. Cover and let rest 10 minutes on lightly floured surface. Prepare Honey Walnut Filling; set aside. Mix 1/4 cup margarine, the brown sugar and honey in ungreased rectangular pan, 13 × 9 × 2 inches; spread evenly in pan.

Roll or pat dough into 24 × 9-inch rectangle. Spread filling crosswise over half of the rectangle to within 1/4 inch of edges of dough; fold dough crosswise in half over filling; seal edges. Cut rectangle crosswise into six 2-inch strips. Twist each strip loosely; place strips crosswise in pan. Cover and let rise in warm place about 1 hour or until double.

Heat oven to 375°. Bake 20 to 25 minutes or until golden brown. Immediately turn pan upside down onto heatproof serving platter. Let pan remain over coffee cake 1 minute; remove pan. Serve warm.

Honey-Walnut Filling

1/2 cup chopped walnuts

1/3 cup margarine or butter, softened

1/4 cup honey

Mix all ingredients.

■ 1 Serving: 365 calories (170 calories from fat); 19g fat (5g saturated); 30mg cholesterol; 350mg sodium; 45g carbohydrate (1g dietary fiber); 5g protein

Potica

1 coffee cake, 10 servings

1/2 cup milk

1/4 cup firm margarine or butter, cut up

1 egg

2 cups bread flour

1/4 cup sugar

1/4 teaspoon salt

1 teaspoon bread machine or quick active dry yeast

Walnut Filling (below)

1 egg white, beaten

Measure carefully, placing all ingredients except Walnut Filling and beaten egg white in bread machine pan in the order recommended by the manufacturer.

Select Dough/Manual cycle. Do not use delay cycles.

Remove dough from pan, using lightly floured hands. Cover and let rest 10 minutes on lightly floured surface. Prepare Walnut Filling.

Grease large cookie sheet. Roll dough into 16 × 12-inch rectangle on lightly floured surface. Spread filling over dough to within 1/2 inch of edges. Roll up tightly, beginning at 16-inch side; pinch edge of dough into roll to seal. Stretch and shape roll until even. Coil roll of dough to form a snail shape. Place on cookie sheet. Cover and let rise in warm place 30 to 60 minutes or until double. (Dough is ready if indentation remains when touched.)

Heat oven to 325°. Brush beaten egg white over dough. Bake 45 to 55 minutes or until golden brown. Remove from cookie sheet to cool.

SHAPING

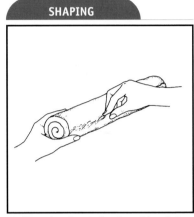

Roll up dough; pinch edge of dough into roll to seal.

Coil roll of dough to form snail shape.

Walnut Filling

2 cups finely chopped or ground walnuts (about 7 ounces)

1/3 cup honey

1/3 cup milk

3 tablespoons sugar

1 egg yolk

Mix all ingredients in medium saucepan. Heat to boiling, stirring frequently, over medium heat. Reduce heat; simmer uncovered 5 minutes, stirring occasionally. Spread in shallow dish; cover and refrigerate until chilled.

■ 1 Serving: 335 calories (145 calories from fat); 16g fat (2g saturated); 45mg cholesterol; 150mg sodium; 43g carbohydrate (2g dietary fiber); 7g protein

Sherried Hazelnut Braid

1 braid, 16 slices

SHAPING

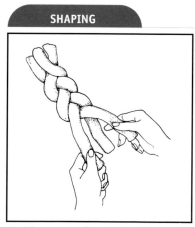

Braid ropes gently and loosely, starting at the middle.

1 cup apple juice

1/4 cup dry sherry or apple juice

4 teaspoons margarine or butter, softened

3 cups bread flour

1/2 cup chopped hazelnuts, toasted (see Success Tip)

3/4 teaspoon salt

1/4 teaspoon ground cinnamon

1 1/4 teaspoons bread machine or quick active dry yeast

1/2 cup golden raisins

1 tablespoon margarine or butter, softened, if desired

Cinnamon Glaze (below)

Measure all ingredients except raisins, 1 tablespoon margarine and Cinnamon Glaze in bread machine pan in the order recommended by the manufacturer. Add raisins at the Raisin/Nut signal.

Select Dough/Manual cycle. Do not use delay cycles.

Remove dough from pan, using lightly floured hands. Cover and let rest 10 minutes on lightly floured surface.

Grease large cookie sheet. Divide dough into thirds. Roll each third into 18-inch rope. Place ropes side by side on cookie sheet; braid together gently and loosely starting at the middle. Pinch ends to fasten. Brush 1 tablespoon margarine over dough. Cover and let rise in warm place 45 to 60 minutes or until double. (Dough is ready if indentation remains when touched.)

Heat oven to 375°. Bake 25 to 30 minutes or until braid is golden brown and sounds hollow when tapped. Remove from cookie sheet to wire rack. Cool completely. Drizzle with Cinnamon Glaze.

■ 1 Slice: 165 calories (35 calories from fat); 4g fat (0g saturated); 0mg cholesterol; 120mg sodium; 30g carbohydrate (1g dietary fiber); 3g protein

Cinnamon Glaze

Mix 1/2 cup powdered sugar, 1 teaspoon dry sherry or apple juice, 1/8 teaspoon ground cinnamon, and 1 to 1 1/2 teaspoons water until smooth and thin enough to drizzle.

Swedish Coffee Ring

1 ring, 16 servings

3/4 cup water

2 eggs

1/4 cup margarine or butter, softened

Pinch of saffron, crushed (see Note below)

4 cups bread flour

1/3 cup sugar

1 teaspoon salt

4 teaspoons bread machine or quick active dry yeast

1/3 cup chopped citron or candied mixed fruit

1/4 cup chopped blanched almonds

2 teaspoons grated lemon peel

Vanilla Glaze (below)

Green and red candied cherries, if desired

Measure all ingredients except citron, almonds, lemon peel, Vanilla Glaze and cherries in bread machine pan in the order recommended by the manufacturer. Add citron, almonds and peel at the Raisin/Nut signal.

Select Dough/Manual cycle. Do not use delay cycles.

Remove dough from pan, using lightly floured hands. Cover and let rest 10 minutes on lightly floured surface.

Grease large cookie sheet. Divide dough in half. Roll each half into 30-inch rope. Place ropes side by side on cookie sheet; twist together gently and loosely. Pinch ends to fasten. Shape twist into a circle on cookie sheet; pinch ends together. Cover and let rise in warm place 45 to 60 minutes or until double.

Heat oven to 375°. Bake 20 to 25 minutes or until golden brown. Remove from cookie sheet. Cool. Drizzle with glaze. Top with cherries.

NOTE: If you don't have saffron, just add two or three drops of yellow food color.

Vanilla Glaze

1 cup powdered sugar

About 1 tablespoon water

1/4 teaspoon vanilla

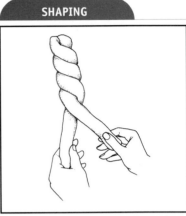
SHAPING

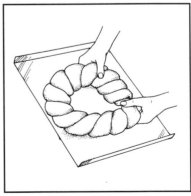

Twist ropes together; pinch ends to fasten.

Shape twist into a circle on cookie sheet; pinch ends together.

Mix ingredients until smooth and thin enough to drizzle.

■ 1 Serving: 230 calories (45 calories from fat); 5g fat (1g saturated); 25mg cholesterol; 109mg sodium; 43g carbohydrate (2g dietary fiber); 5g protein

Crunchy Wheat and Honey Twist

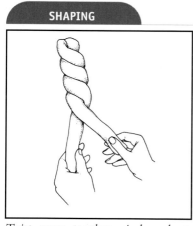

Twist ropes together; pinch ends to fasten.

1 twist, 16 slices

3/4 cup plus 2 tablespoons water

2 tablespoons honey

1 tablespoon margarine or butter, softened

1 1/4 cups whole wheat flour

1 cup bread flour

1/3 cup slivered almonds, toasted (page 59)

1 teaspoon salt

1 teaspoon bread machine or quick active dry yeast

Margarine or butter, melted, if desired

1 egg, slightly beaten

2 tablespoons sugar

1/4 teaspoon ground cinnamon

Measure carefully, placing all ingredients except melted margarine, egg, sugar and cinnamon in bread machine pan in the order recommended by the manufacturer.

Select Dough/Manual cycle. Do not use delay cycles.

Remove dough from pan, using lightly floured hands. Cover and let rest 10 minutes on lightly floured surface.

Grease large cookie sheet. Divide dough in half. Roll each half into 15-inch rope. Place ropes side by side on cookie sheet; twist together gently and loosely. Pinch ends to fasten. Brush melted margarine lightly over dough. Cover and let rise in warm place 45 to 60 minutes or until double. (Dough is ready if indentation remains when touched.)

Heat oven to 375°. Brush egg over dough. Mix sugar and cinnamon; sprinkle over dough. Bake 25 to 30 minutes or until twist is golden brown and sounds hollow when tapped. Remove from cookie sheet to wire rack; cool.

■ 1 Slice: 95 calories (20 calories from fat); 2g fat (1g saturated); 15mg cholesterol; 160mg sodium; 18g carbohydrate (2g dietary fiber); 3g protein

Sweet Bread Wreath

1 wreath, 24 servings

1/4 cup water

3/4 cup sour cream

1 egg

3 cups bread flour

3 tablespoons sugar

1 teaspoon salt

2 teaspoons bread machine or quick active dry yeast

1 egg, beaten

3 tablespoons sugar

1/4 teaspoon ground cinnamon

1/4 teaspoon ground anise or ground cloves

1/4 teaspoon freshly grated or ground nutmeg

Measure carefully, placing all ingredients except beaten egg, 3 tablespoons sugar, the cinnamon, anise and nutmeg in bread machine pan in the order recommended by the manufacturer.

Select Dough/Manual cycle. Do not use delay cycles.

Remove dough from pan, using lightly floured hands. Cover and let rest 10 minutes on lightly floured surface.

Grease large cookie sheet. Divide dough into thirds. Roll each third into 26-inch rope. Place ropes side by side; braid together gently and loosely. Pinch ends to fasten. Shape braid into circle on cookie sheet; pinch ends together. Cover and let rise in warm place 45 to 50 minutes or until double. (Dough is ready if indentation remains when touched.)

Heat oven to 350°. Brush beaten egg over dough. Mix 3 tablespoons sugar, the cinnamon, anise and nutmeg; sprinkle over dough. Bake 25 to 30 minutes or until golden brown.

■ 1 Serving: 80 calories (20 calories from fat); 2g fat (1g saturated); 20mg cholesterol; 105mg sodium; 14g carbohydrate (0g dietary fiber); 2g protein

SHAPING

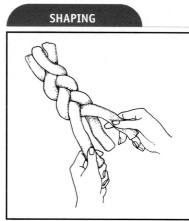

Braid ropes gently and loosely, starting at the middle.

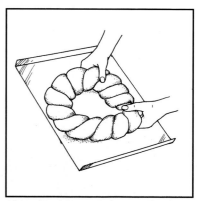

Shape braid into a circle on cookie sheet; pinch ends together.

Sweet Bread Wreath

Bread Baking Glossary

We hope this glossary will be helpful when you use your Betty Crocker cookbook, purchase bread from a bakery or supermarket or just want to learn more about the wonderful world of bread baking.

Bagel: A doughnut-shaped roll made from flour, water, salt and yeast. It is shaped, raised, boiled and then baked.

Baguette: A long, thin bread with diagonal slashes on the top, a crispy, golden brown outside and a chewy, open-textured interior. In French, the word baguette means "wand."

Baking stone: Also known as pizza stone or bread stone, a thin piece of porous, unglazed stone or baking tile that distributes heat evenly and absorbs the moisture in bread dough. The result is a crisp, crusty bread. Place the stone in the oven, and then preheat the oven; a cold stone in a hot oven may cause the stone to crack. Sprinkle cornmeal on the heated stone, and slide the dough onto the stone.

Bâtarde or Bâtard: Medium-long loaf that is wide in the center and tapered at both ends. Also called a French loaf.

Boule: French word for "ball," and that is what it is—a fat, round loaf of bread.

Brioche: Light yeast dough rich with butter and eggs, this French creation is an elegant bread. It can be made in the classic shape, called *brioche à tête,* which has a fluted bottom and a topknot baked in a golden loaf. Brioche can be a loaf or individual rolls.

Bromated: See potassium bromate.

Bulgur wheat: Also known as bulghur, bulgar or burghul. Consists of wheat kernels that have been steamed, dried and crushed. It is available in coarse, medium and fine grinds.

Challah: Rich egg-and-butter yeast dough. It is traditionally braided and is the symbol of the Jewish Sabbath. It should be a little sweet and have a soft texture.

Chop: To cut into coarse or fine irregular pieces, using a knife, chopper, blender or food processor.

Ciabatta: Italian word for "old slipper." An irregular-shaped Italian flatbread that is dusted with flour. The dough is "dimpled" with the fingers before it is baked; the indentations are characteristic of this bread.

Citron: A semitropical fruit that looks like an oversized, lumpy lemon. It is very sour and not eaten raw. The thick peel is candied and used in baking.

Corn flour: Finely ground cornmeal; can be used with wheat flour in baking. *Masa harina* is a special corn flour that is used for making tortillas.

Corn syrup: Clear, thick liquid (dark or light are interchangeable in recipes) made from corn sugar mixed with acid.

Cornmeal: Dried corn kernels ground into either fine, medium or coarse texture. Water-ground, also known as stone-ground, is the old-fashioned method of using water power to turn the mill wheels. Some of the hull and germ is retained, so this cornmeal is more nutritious. A newer method of milling is done by huge steel rollers that remove the most of the hull and germ. Water- or stone-ground is usually labeled as such, but steel-ground is seldom indicated on the label.

Couronne: Large, doughnut-shaped loaf of bread. The dough is shaped into a circle, then the baker pushes an elbow into the center to make a hole. The hole is then enlarged by shaping with the fingers. After the dough has risen, the hole is made square using the handle of a wooden spoon, or a circle is cut in the dough an inch or two from the center hole.

Dough scraper: Square piece of metal that has a sharp edge and a wooden or turned metal handle on the other side. It is used for scraping dough off the work surface during kneading or for cutting dough into pieces. It is also handy for cleaning up the flour and dough that is left on the work area.

Dried fruit: Fruit that has most of the moisture removed. Dried fruits have a more concentrated sweetness and flavor. Use dried fruits that are still moist. If they are too old and dried, they will absorb moisture from the dough or may stay in hard little pieces in the baked product. Dried-out fruits can be plumped by soaking in liquid or by steaming.

Drizzle: To pour in thin lines from a spoon or liquid measuring cup in an uneven pattern over food.

Dust: Sprinkle lightly with flour, cornmeal, powdered sugar or baking cocoa.

Epi: French loaf of bread that is cut with a pair of small sharp scissors so it resembles a wheat stalk. Cuts are made diagonally about 2 inches apart on the top of the loaf, cutting almost three-fourths of the way into the loaf. A cut piece is lifted and turned to the right; the next piece is lifted and turned to the left, until all pieces have been turned to alternating sides.

Flour: See Know Your Bread Ingredients, page 8.

Focaccia: Italian flatbread that can be shaped into a large round or rectangle. It is "dimpled" by pressing with the fingers, drizzled or brushed with olive oil and sprinkled with salt. Other ingredients and herbs can be added to the top before baking.

Fougasse: A decorative flatbread that originated in Provence, France. After the dough is flattened, slashes are made and spread open to resemble a leaf, tree, sun or any decorative design.

Glaze: To brush, spread or drizzle an ingredient or mixture of ingredients onto hot or cold foods to give a glossy appearance or hard finish.

Graham flour: Whole wheat flour that is named after Sylvester Graham, who created the milling process for grinding the complete wheat kernel. It is a coarser-ground flour than regular whole wheat.

Grate: To make tiny particles by rubbing a hard-textured food against the small, rough, sharp-edge holes of a grater.

Grease: To rub the inside surface of a bowl or pan with shortening or oil, using a pastry brush, waxed paper or paper towel, to prevent food from sticking to it.

Grissini: Italian breadsticks. They can be long and pencil thin or thicker and knobby.

Julekage: Sweet bread that is full of fruits and flavored with cardamom. A popular Christmas treat in Denmark, Sweden and Norway.

Kasha: Roasted buckwheat kernels or groats, often called kasha, that are the hulled seeds of the buckwheat plant.

Knead: To work dough on a floured surface into a smooth, elastic mass, using hands or an electric mixer with dough hooks or a cycle in the bread machine. Kneading develops the gluten in flour, which results in an even texture and smooth, rounded top. It can take up to about 15 minutes by hand.

Kosher salt: A coarse-grain salt with no additives.

Kuchen: German word for "cake," it is a yeast coffee cake that has a fruit or cheese topping.

Lame: Single-edged razor blade that is used to make decorative slashes in the tops of bread dough before baking. A sharp, thin knife or finely serrated knife also works. Sharp scissors can be used but can sometime leave "snip marks" in the slashed line.

Millet: Ancient grass that has a small, round yellow seed that can be ground and used like flour in cakes, breads and puddings.

Oat bran: The outer casing of the oat; high in soluble fiber and thought to help reduce high cholesterol.

Oat flour: Made from oat groats that have been ground into powder. It contains no gluten-forming protein, so it must be used with wheat or bread flour for yeast breads.

Oats: Oat groats are whole oats that have been cleaned, toasted, hulled and cleaned again. Oat groats become rolled oats, also known as old-fashioned oats, when they have been steamed and flattened with huge rollers. Quick-cooking rolled oats have been cut into several pieces before being steamed and rolled into thinner flakes so they cook faster. Instant oats have been precooked and dried before rolling, so they cannot be used interchangeably with rolled or quick-cooking rolled oats.

Panettone: Sweet yeast bread studded with fruit and nuts that originated in Milan, Italy. It is baked in a tall, cylindrical shape that reminded Italians of cathedral domes. It traditionally is served at Christmastime but also at other celebrations such as weddings and christenings.

Panini: Italian rolls, available in various shapes.

Pastry brush: Small brush used for applying egg washes, glazes or melted margarine or butter on breads and pastries before or after baking. Softer bristles are best for yeast doughs and delicate pastries.

Pastry wheel: Small sharp cutting wheel that is attached to a handle; used for marking or cutting pastry or cookie dough.

Peel: 1. To cut off outer covering, using knife or vegetable peeler. Also, to strip off outer covering, using fingers. 2. Flat smooth wooden or metal paddle with a long handle used to slide yeast breads and pizza in and out of ovens. Also known as a baker's peel.

Petits pains: French hard rolls that are crusty on the outside and soft and tender inside.

Potassium bromate: Used to quickly improve the baking performance of flour. Freshly milled flour may not make consistently high-quality baked products, so it must be stored for several months in order that natural oxidation occurs. The oxidation produces whiter flour and results in flour with a finer texture and improved baking quality. Potassium bromate is sometimes added to high-protein wheat flours to quickly improve the baking performance and make baked products with better volume and crumb structure. Flours containing potassium bromate are required to be labeled "bromated."

Pumpernickel: Coarse dark bread with a slightly sour taste. It is made with rye and wheat flours and often has molasses and baking cocoa added for flavor and color.

Punch down: To push out the accumulated gases in yeast dough after it has risen, either by gently pushing the fist into it, or by gently folding the dough over several times using the hands.

Retardation: The stage when dough is put in a cool place (but not cold enough to kill the yeast), such as a refrigerator, to retard or inhibit the yeast. This gives the dough time to develop its flavor.

Rising: To cover yeast dough and place it in a draft-free place so the yeast can ferment. Also called proofing.

Rye flour: Milled from the whole rye berry; usually found as medium-ground in most supermarkets. Although it is high in protein, it is low in the two gluten-forming proteins. Therefore, rye flour is generally mixed with wheat flour for making breads with good texture and volume.

Scald: To heat liquid to just below the boiling point. Tiny bubbles will form at the edge. A thin skin will form on the top of milk.

Score: To cut the surface of food about 1/4 inch deep, using a sharp knife or single-edge razor blade, to facilitate cooking or baking or for appearance.

Sea salt: Made from evaporating sea water; has a pure and natural taste.

Shred: To cut into long, thin pieces, using round, smooth holes of shredder, knife or food processor.

Slice: To cut into uniform-size flat pieces.

Sponge: A starter that usually is a mix of yeast, some liquid and flour, set aside to rise before the remaining ingredients are added. The sponge can be made in the bread machine pan; close the lid and let the sponge work

before adding the remaining ingredients.

Starter: A premix for yeast dough. It can be a sourdough starter, a chef or a sponge. It may contain a commercial yeast, or for sourdough or a chef, a wild or naturally fermented yeast. A simple starter is made by mixing flour and water with a pinch of commercial yeast and letting it become a bubbly mixture. Feed the starter and let it stand over a period of days or weeks; it will attract airborne yeast in your own kitchen.

Stirato: Long, thin Italian bread. The dough can be "stretched" to make as long a loaf as will fit into your oven.

Stollen: German sweet bread studded with candied fruits and nuts. It can be braided or folded over and is dusted with powdered sugar after baking.

Stone-ground: Process for grinding whole wheat flour that crushes the kernel between two slowly moving stones, so the endosperm and germ are included in the flour.

Straight rise: Refers to yeast dough that is made without a starter. The dough is mixed, rises one or two times, is shaped and baked. The breads in our cookbook are straight rise except for the two sourdough loaves.

Table salt: A fine-grained refined salt that is required by the FDA to be washed free of its trace minerals and magnesium. This salt is mainly used for cooking and as a condiment on the table.

Triticale: Grain that is a cross of wheat with rye. Triticale flour is higher in protein than other nonwheat flours but still needs to be combined with a wheat flour to produce a satisfying texture.

Torpedo: A popular bread shape in both Italy and France, it is a cigar-shaped loaf that is tapered at both ends like a torpedo.

Wheat berry: The whole unprocessed wheat kernel; contains the bran, endosperm and germ.

Wheat bran: The rough outer covering of the wheat berry; has very little nutritional value except for fiber. It is removed during milling.

Wheat germ: The sprouting segment of the wheat berry that contains the fat. It is removed from all flours except from whole wheat flour. It can be purchased either powdered or whole and can be added to bread doughs.

Yeast: See Know Your Bread Ingredients, page 8.

Helpful Nutrition and Baking Information

Nutrition Guidelines

We provide nutrition information for each recipe that includes calories, fat, cholesterol, sodium, carbohydrate, fiber and protein. Individual food choices can be based on this information.

Recommended intake for a daily diet of 2,000 calories as set by the Food and Drug Administration.

Total Fat	Less than 65g
Saturated Fat	Less than 20g
Cholesterol	Less than 300mg
Sodium	Less than 2,400mg
Total Carbohydrate	300g
Dietary Fiber	25g

Criteria Used for Calculating Nutrition Information

- The first ingredient was used wherever a choice is given (such as 1/3 cup sour cream or plain yogurt).

- The first ingredient amount was used wherever a range is given (such as 3 to 3 1/2-pound cut-up broiler-fryer chicken).

- The first serving number was used wherever a range is given (such as 4 to 6 servings).

- "If desired" ingredients (such as sprinkle with brown sugar if desired) and recipe variations were *not* included.

- Only the amount of a marinade or frying oil that is estimated to be absorbed by the food during preparation or cooking was calculated.

Ingredients Used in Recipe Testing and Nutrition Calculations

- Ingredients used for testing represent those that the majority of consumers use in their homes: large eggs, 2% milk, 80% lean ground beef, canned ready-to-use chicken broth, and vegetable oil spread containing *not less than 65 percent fat.*

- Fat-free, low-fat or low-sodium products are not used, unless otherwise indicated.

- Solid vegetable shortening (not butter, margarine, nonstick cooking sprays or vegetable oil spread as they can cause sticking problems) is used to grease pans, unless otherwise indicated.

Equipment Used in Recipe Testing

We use equipment for testing that the majority of consumers use in their homes. If a specific piece of equipment (such as a wire whisk) is necessary for recipe success, it will be listed in the recipe.

- Cookware and bakeware **without** nonstick coatings were used, unless otherwise indicated.

- No dark colored, black or insulated bakeware was used.

- When a baking pan is specified in a recipe, a *metal* pan was used; a baking dish or pie plate means oven-proof glass was used.

- An electric hand mixer was used for mixing *only when mixer speeds are specified* in the recipe directions. When a mixer speed is not given, a spoon or fork was used.

Metric Conversion Guide

Volume

U.S. Units	Canadian Metric	Australian Metric
1/4 teaspoon	1 mL	1 ml
1/2 teaspoon	2 mL	2 ml
1 teaspoon	5 mL	5 ml
1 tablespoon	15 mL	20 ml
1/4 cup	50 mL	60 ml
1/3 cup	75 mL	80 ml
1/2 cup	125 mL	125 ml
2/3 cup	150 mL	170 ml
3/4 cup	175 mL	190 ml
1 cup	250 mL	250 ml
1 quart	1 liter	1 liter
1 1/2 quarts	1.5 liters	1.5 liters
2 quarts	2 liters	2 liters
2 1/2 quarts	2.5 liters	2.5 liters
3 quarts	3 liters	3 liters
4 quarts	4 liters	4 liters

Weight

U.S. Units	Canadian Metric	Australian Metric
1 ounce	30 grams	30 grams
2 ounces	55 grams	60 grams
3 ounces	85 grams	90 grams
4 ounces (1/4 pound)	115 grams	125 grams
8 ounces (1/2 pound)	225 grams	225 grams
16 ounces (1 pound)	455 grams	500 grams
1 pound	455 grams	1/2 kilogram

Note: The recipes in this cookbook have not been developed or tested using metric measures. When converting recipes to metric, some variations in quality may be noted.

Measurements

Inches	Centimeters
1	2.5
2	5.0
3	7.5
4	10.0
5	12.5
6	15.0
7	17.5
8	20.5
9	23.0
10	25.5
11	28.0
12	30.5
13	33.0

Temperatures

Fahrenheit	Celsius
32°	0°
212°	100°
250°	120°
275°	140°
300°	150°
325°	160°
350°	180°
375°	190°
400°	200°
425°	220°
450°	230°
475°	240°
500°	260°

Index